Too Funny for Words

TOO FUNNY

FOR WORDS

Backstage Tales from Broadway, Television, and the Movies

JERRY ADLER

VIVA
EDITIONS

Published in the United States by Viva Editions, an imprint of Start Midnight, LLC, 221 River Street, Ninth Floor, Hoboken, New Jersey 07030.

Printed in the United States
Cover design: Jennifer Do
Cover photo: Joan Adler
Cover image: Shutterstock / New Africa, Roman Medvid
Cover image: Cover photo: Joan Adler, Shutterstock / New Africa, Roman Medvid
Text design: Frank Wiedemann

First Edition.
10 9 8 7 6 5 4 3 2 1

Trade paper ISBN: 978-1-63228-096-1
E-book ISBN: 978-1-63228-120-3

To Joan:

Without your encouragement, exuberance, and fabulous good taste,
none of this happy event would have taken place.
What wonderful times we have had, and I owe so much to you.
Much love and gratitude.

Special Thanks

Alex Ephraim, our wondrous and patient editor
(but dear friend too).

Ian Kleinert, our intrepid agent.

David Bernhardt of davidsgraphica.com whose
genius creativity made this book special.
You never know who you will meet walking your dog!

Marlene Adler for spending all the time organizing
photo and studio data, without whom this book
would never have been finished.

AUTHOR'S STATEMENT

This is an anecdotal memoir. It is a kind of a remembrance of things past from the seventy-plus years of my show business career. Spanning Broadway, Television, and the Movies, I detail my personal interactions with many of the well-known figures I've worked with from Marilyn Monroe to Meryl Streep.

TABLE OF CONTENTS

Orson Welles. Marilyn Monroe. Milton Berle. George S. Kaufman. Zero Mostel. Ira Gershwin.

"What is a 'Jerry Adler'?"
—ORSON WELLES

Anyone could recognize that voice, even on a phone call from Rome. It had been arranged by Orson Welles's agent that I call him at the Grand Hotel at 10 a.m. his time, 4 a.m. my time. I called. He answered. No matter how prepared you are, it's 4 a.m, you're in your underwear, dry-throated, and terribly nervous at making a good impression on one of your great heroes and, damn it, the call goes through. I explained, sounding as important as I could, getting a little moisture in my vocal cords, that I was interested in producing his play, *Moby Dick—Rehearsed*, on Broadway. I must have thrown him a curve because there was a deafening silence at the other end of the call. All I could hear was my own bated breath. What the hell, I jumped in and told him I was Jerry Adler, a stage manager in New York currently working on *My Fair Lady*, and that I had read the London reviews of his play and wanted to bring it over.

I suppose out of sheer pity he said, "You're out of your fucking mind, but let's talk. How soon can you get here? I hate the telephone and I'm on a tight schedule."

Rome? I didn't have the proper wallet, so how would I find a way to buy a ticket to Italy? I did have a partner in this venture, but I sensed Welles was drifting away and I certainly couldn't rouse anyone at this hour.

I vacillated a second and then put my foot in my mouth, "See you on Sunday, OK?"

He said, "I'll be in the bar from ten on." *Click*!

My partner in this crazy idea was Samuel Liff—everyone called him "Biff" for reasons of rhyme, I guess. He was production stage manager on *My Fair Lady*, and I was his assistant. He was also floored when I broke the news of my Sunday go-to-meeting offer and Welles's expectation that we meet not too far from Vatican City. We had four days to scrape up the cash and thank God we had a flush company manager, Sam Schwartz, who amazingly put up the seed money for a piece of the show. I got elected to go because Biff had to keep the home fires burning back at the Hellinger Theatre, so the "game was afoot." And what the hell, if that old timer, stage manager Bobby Griffith, and his partner/assistant Hal Prince could do it with *The Pajama Game* why couldn't we with our whale of a show?

I flew on the Saturday before my meeting with Orson—see, I'm calling him by his first name already just like a regular producer! All I needed now was a contract for the rights and a big cigar. I took so much Valium, my memory of the flight is a little vague. All I do remember was the realization that I was meeting Citizen

Kane, face-to-face. Would I handle it right, appear confident and knowledgeable? How the hell did I get into this mess? He was at the bar the next morning as he said he would be, but I wouldn't have recognized him except for that familiar, fabulous voice. There he was, corpulent, unshaven, and smoking what looked like a knockwurst. Entertaining the patrons with imperious gusto, he was the perfect Captain Ahab.

I wasn't sure what to do, so I just waved, and he promptly announced to all, "Ah, here's my Broadway producer!"

Well, the producer and his star spent most of the day bantering back and forth about how terrific *Moby Dick—Rehearsed* was in London and how much he was looking forward to seeing *My Fair Lady*. He even got me to promise house seats when he got to New York. It was getting late, and I was feeling the effects of gin and tonic before breakfast, but every time I brought out Sam Schwartz's deal memo, he ordered another round. He finally invited me to dinner, announced his departure, and left. The only appeal dinner had was the prospect of his signature on my contract, and dessert. We met in the Palm Court after I had napped and pulled myself together letting all that booze aerate. He was at a table with the best-looking woman I had seen in Rome. Orson introduced me—I have no recollection of her name, my mind was elsewhere—and proceeded to interview the lady. I kind of gathered he was intending to film *Macbeth* or *Chimes at Midnight*. I could hardly keep up since the hangover was peaking in my brain. Eventually he rose. I think I was having soup at the time, in honor of the old Hebraic mantra, "If you're sick, have some chicken soup." Excusing himself, he left me alone with the hopeful Lady Macbeth who, by the way, was totally incoherent in English. Since Welles had introduced me as his "Broadway producer" to the lady, God love her, did her level best to showcase her attributes which were extensive and enticing even in a language lost on me. After what seemed the end of time, the *maître d'* came over, excused himself and whispered that Mr. Welles needed me. He assured me that Mr. Welles wasn't ill but asked that I follow him. I did and found Welles sitting on a huge throne-like chair beside the men's room, smoking another knockwurst.

"Get rid of her for me, will you? Tell her I got beriberi in the men's room. Tell her anything but get her out. I'm not leaving this chair until she's gone. You're a big Broadway guy, tell her she's great and goodnight," he said.

Embarrassingly, I did just that, escorted her out, had black coffee and waited for "The Singing." Instead, I got a note saying he was tired but would meet me at the front desk at 9 a.m. He wasn't at the front desk at 9 a.m., or at 9:30 a.m. either; all there was, finally as I checked the desk, was the information that Mr. Welles had checked out but had left a note for Mr. Adler which read, "Have an early call, but I've left a company car for you at the Zagreb Airport. See you there and we'll chat," signed, Welles. Where the fuck is Zagreb? How could I get there, should I even try? I called Biff and we mutually mourned how deep we were treading in the stush, but Biff was positive, realizing we had come this far, and Welles seemed close to signing. The concierge was terrific and got me to the airport where my meager budget flew me to Zagreb, which turned out to be in Yugoslavia and just across the Adriatic. The ticket would eventually get me back to New York if I lived that long. The car was indeed waiting for me with a mammoth Yugo holding a card scrawled with my name. The guy spoke as much English as the lady in Rome and it increasingly dawned on me that if he dropped me anywhere, I was dead as a doornail. But fate left me at a tent on a movie set in the middle of nowhere, greeting Genghis Khan in his shorts, still smoking that hideous cigar. He apologized for dragging me a million miles to "this crazy place," but having thought it over, he would be delighted to have me produce his play in New York for no other reason than the resilience I'd shown. Man, I whipped that deal memo under his nose so fast, he didn't even read the thing while he signed it. He flourished it in the air and pronounced it "the Magna Carta" while handing it to me with the enclosed check still attached. I was to send the check to his agent in London who would do all the legal rigamarole. The only bad news was, as he tore up the actor agreement, he would not appear in the play. I pleaded the case noting that his appearance on Broadway would generate tremendous box office and would certainly put the project on page one. I was blowing his horn as loud as I could, but to no avail.

"I'll never play anything in New York while that son of a bitch Taubman is the critic at the *Times*!"

He was still raving as the Cossacks pulled him away. I was absolutely amazed that I had the signed paper in my hands. Incredibly, I never saw him again. The giant Yugo got me back to Zagreb and I made it home to a somewhat cheerful reception. What the hell, we raised the capital by strong-arming everyone we knew, getting the Schubert's to give us the Barrymore Theatre, signing Douglas Campbell, a fabulous Canadian director from the Royal Shakespeare Theatre, and casting most of the principals from that illustrious company. We then announced that Rod Steiger would play Ahab. The rehearsals were a joy, our names on the marquee of the Barrymore were a hoot, and all went well. We were PRODUCERS! Opening night was electric and the company was great playing to a standing ovation. Of course, Welles was right, Taubman panned him and greeted the play with a yawn, but the other notices were good, like those from Anthony Cookman, calling it "A whale of a show!"[1] We opened in November, but without the *Times* and Orson himself, we closed in December.

---

1 Cookman, Anthony. 1955. "Whale of a Show." *Tatler & Bystander*, June 29, 1955.

* * *

I've been telling stories like that for years, entertaining friends and family, and shrugging off the idea that I should "write a book." The pandemic, with months of isolation looming, finally pushed me to a blank page on my computer. It quickly became a joy remembering all the good times.

This isn't a memoir.

Memoirs are autobiographical and delve into births, families, dates, etc. I can't remember what I did last Thursday, let alone February 4, 1929. What this is is a collection of events I'd like to share, experiences I'd like to put down on paper. It's mostly about people, living or dead, actually actual, famous or kind of infamous. The book involves a life in theatre, television, and the movies, simply because, that's all I've ever done

Pardon, I have to divert for some special family lore I learned at my father's knee. My father was Phil Adler, reputed to be the fastest and funniest General Manager in the business (more about him later). Here it is:

I come from a long line of Adlers. Louie Adler arrived at Ellis Island at the turn of the century . . . broke. His cousin from the well-to-do Russian side of the family tree was Jacob Adler, a famous actor. He had a theater on the lower east side of New York City where Shakespeare was performed in Yiddish. Jacob, from Austria, had children, Stella and Luther, who became famous actors. Louie, who quickly met and married my grandmother, had four sons, the last of whom was Philip, my father, who sold ties as a young boy during the Great Depression. It was said, when Louie, the tailor, asked Jacob, the actor, for a loan, he came away with a ticket to *King Lear*.

One rainy and thundering night when I was five or six, a huge clap of thunder woke me and, frightened, I headed for my parent's bedroom. We had rented a room to a couple, and I tried not to wake them as I passed through. Of course, I had no idea my parents were in the middle of some passionate sex. I patted my father on the shoulder and he howled through the storm:

"Oh, my God. I almost had a heart attack. What do you want? Are you okay?"

"I'm scared. Can I come sleep in the bed with you and mommy?"

He quickly said, "I'm sorry, son. Can't you see how crowded it is? I have to sleep on top of mommy." Even the renters were laughing.

Pretty fast retort at a moment like that. My father, Phil, was the company manager of the Group Theatre, that fervent hotbed of original theater where all the Adlers seemed to end up. But more importantly, he was the king of nepotism. Sadly, or kind of opportunistically, I was expelled from Syracuse University for ignoring classes and spending all my time at the Boar's Head Playhouse, where I directed, acted, built scenery, and spent most of my days having the time of my life. Admittedly, he was probably happy to stop paying the tuition of six hundred dollars a year, including room and board in Quonset huts put up at the end of World War II, not exactly a bargain in 1949. An opening occurred on *Gentlemen Prefer Blondes* for an assistant stage manager, and since my father was general manager, off I went into a lifetime of what was then called "show business."

I started on Labor Day, 1950 at a salary of thirty-five dollars a week, which was terrific since I lived in a tiny penthouse on New York's West Side, for forty-nine dollars a month. The show had been running like clockwork for six months at the Ziegfeld Theatre, a gorgeous building fronting 54th Street and 6th Avenue which they inexplicably tore down later to make way for the Ziegfeld Movie Theatre. The show had an enormous cast of sixty performers, and because of the incompetence of the guy I replaced, my job was extraordinarily minimal. It was making sure the dozen showgirls were on in time (they had a tendency to play canasta up in their room), chatting with Charles "Honi" Coles, a fabulous dancer and raconteur, and, most importantly, leading Carol Channing around with a flashlight since she was extraordinarily nearsighted. It was a gas to see her check the bulletin board, her nose touching the wall. The best part was learning the ropes from Frank Coletti, the boss, and his assistant, Biff, who became a lifelong friend and mentor. The whole thing was a classroom filled with gorgeous women, funny guys, and Carol, who would have ended up in the orchestra pit if it wasn't for me.

The most menial job was the money box. In those days, everyone in the cast was paid in cash on Friday night. The money box was given to me during "half-hour" by my father and a security person holding pay envelopes, with names attached, which I disseminated before the show began and during intermission. It certainly was an archaic way of doing things, but that was common on Broadway in those days. It reminded me of the day my father took me to work when I was about twelve years old. He was company manager of *Tobacco Road,* a notorious play full of "adulterous sex and blasphemous language"[2] according to Brock Pemberton, which ran from 1933 until 1941 and put food on the Adler table from the Depression until Pearl Harbor. It was a shocking play, especially when Henry Hull, playing the lead, urinated on stage, startling the audience and me. Anyway, after the performance, my father sat at a little table on stage and paid the cast, who had lined up, in cash. The ubiquitous money box held sway until the mid 1950s when, of all people, Phil Adler had things changed. Knowing *My Fair Lady* was the most successful production on Broadway and wanting to establish his company as a commanding banking enterprise, my father offered to do the weekly payroll if it was paid by check.

2 Schildcrout, Jordan. 2019. *In the Long Run: A Cultural History of Broadway's Hit Plays.* London, England: Taylor & Francis. pp. 41–42.

Actors Equity and a majority of the cast agreed if the checks were paid on Thursday instead of the usual Friday. It worked, saving managers a lot of work, giving actors guaranteed salaries, and boosting a little burgeoning New Jersey company called ADT, American District Telegraph.

Frank Berle was his brother Milton's manager and my father's gin-playing buddy. So when Milton Berle decided to do a musical, Frank recommended Phil and, of course, king nepotism got me on staff. Bob Downing, Elia Kazan's favorite stage manager, had been set even though Bob had never done a musical. Now that *Gentlemen Prefer Blondes* was slowing down, I jumped at the chance to do one from the beginning. This was during the time when there were no computers, laptops, or smartphones, nothing that could ease the burden of keeping the Prompt Script totally correct. Corrections had to be typed on mimeo paper and copies made on a mimeograph machine. Those copies had to be disseminated to the full company daily. Since I was the assistant stage manager those jobs fell to me. Additionally, I made the calls and kept the log. It was a great deal to learn but being on a new musical was entirely energizing. Casting went well. I became acutely aware of the sound of "NEXT . . ." from out front. It's that disappointing rejection you hear all too often from the voice in the black void. I came to know it and hate its unfeeling call.

I also found myself involved in problems I had never experienced before. It seemed the director, Hassard Short, who had some great credits like *Show Boat* and *Carmen Jones,* was now totally inebriated, incapable of conversation or discussion after 3 p.m. The playwright, Sally Benson, a renowned screenwriter, had adapted the script from the works of Booth Tarkington, and was now sitting, smiling, and agreeing with anyone and everything. If we were to get this thing on its feet, we needed help. From out of nowhere came Richard Whorf, a notable film actor, who took over as director and handled the situation beautifully. We were booked into the Broadhurst Theatre, one of the Shubert's prime houses. We had an excellent cast with Kenneth Nelson and Anne Crowley, both young but experienced and talented players, as the leads. Frank Albertson, who had played the rich friend to James Stewart in *It's a Wonderful Life*, took on one of the fathers in the show. The other father was to be played by Dennis King, a real Broadway veteran. The score was very lively, and the lyrics were by Kim Gannon. Only one problem existed: the script by Ms. Benson gave you diabetes. Nobody seemed to care, "Uncle Milty" dropped in now and then, drooling over the bevy of nubiles prancing about, smoking his cigar and smiling, smiling like he knew better than anyone that we'd be a hit. Frank Albertson, who became a close friend full of Hollywood anecdotes, faced reality and took a short-term lease on his apartment. Nobody could fix the thing, we had Whorf and Dania Krupska, our young and talented choreographer, doing their best with no help from the somnambulists out front. To everyone's amazement the opening night audience seemed to enjoy the production. And obviously the theater gods were on our side, so we got glowing reviews. The result: it ran for almost a year. Go figure.

Bob Downing left after a few months because he had been summoned by Elia Kazan to assist him. Bob had told me Kazan needed him to take care of his "little idiosyncrasies." It reminded me of stories about George S. Kaufman who also had "little idiosyncrasies;" he hated to be touched and let no one sit behind him during rehearsals. Working for either he or Kazan would be a three-year course in directing at any university. Crazily, it was decided to take the show on the road, with me as production stage manager, hoping that the story of two teenage lovers facing life among the cornflowers would fare well in the hinterlands. Well, we closed after two weeks in Philadelphia. Hayseed is hayseed.

No sooner had I arrived back home from the closing of *Seventeen*, the phone rang. Chandler Cowles, an actor from *Call Me Mister*, a musical about returning GIs from WWII that my father had managed, was doing a revival of George S. Kaufman's *Of Thee I Sing* and offered an assistant stage manager's spot to me. I'm telling you, between networking and nepotism, I hadn't missed a payday since I left college. In the fifties, there was no theater man more admired than Mr. Kaufman, and the idea of being around him and Ira Gershwin, the lyricist of his brother George's score, was terrific. Even though Mr. K treated Joe Olney, the top manager, and me like coworkers, I had trouble keeping a semblance of poise whenever I was near him. He even took us to lunch at the Algonquin when there was a break in auditions at the Belasco Theatre up the street. One such day, we entered the lobby just as the elevator doors opened and Bea Kaufman emerged on the arm of a tall, good-looking guy in a huge cowboy hat. I knew she was George's ex because of the gossip columns screaming headlines about their scandalous divorce. It seems Mr. K was indeed quite a ladies' man.

"Hello there, George," she said, just as we passed by. She introduced the fellow, but I have no recollection of his name. Mr. K just stared at them with an imperious glance. "He's in cotton, you know, George," she grinned, clutching his arm.

Kaufman's immediate response was, "And them that plants 'em, are soon forgotten."

The lyrics from "Ol' Man River," written by Oscar Hammerstein II,[3] were the perfect put-down. The cowboy didn't get it, but

---

3 Paul Whiteman and His Concert Orchestra with Paul Robeson and Mixed Chorus. 1927. "Ol' Man River." B. Harms Co.

Joe and I did. I tried to stifle a laugh but failed and Ira Gershwin almost fell out of his chair when I told him the story. I loved Mr. Gershwin, he reminded me of my grandfather: tiny, humorous, and warm-hearted.

We had a terrific cast headed by Jack Carson, a well-known Hollywood actor, and Paul Hartman, a performer famously known for a dance act with his wife, Grace. James McCracken was in the chorus, later to make an extraordinary career as a leading tenor at the Metropolitan Opera. Michael King was also in the cast and would eventually join me in *My Fair Lady* as Freddy Eynsford-Hill. There were forty people in the show, all of us respectful of the famous people at the helm and of the material we were rehearsing, material that had won the first Pulitzer Prize in Drama.

I had a kind of feeling of nostalgia even while I was doing the work because I knew my number in the Korean War draft was coming up and I had little chance of making it to opening night. In the middle of everything, I was drafted into the Army. By bus I wound up at Fort Pickett, Virginia, and due to my prowess as a typist, I sat at the company desk as my fellow recruits marched off carrying stretchers to basic training (we were in the Medical Corps). It was there, three weeks later that an official notice arrived ordering me to Fort Dix in Wrightstown, New Jersey. My orders directed me to report to, I kid you not, First Lt. Romeo St. Pierre. It seems, I learned as I met him, that this group was Special Services and they were planning a production of *Call Me Mister* (the same show that I had mentioned before *Of Thee I Sing*), a recent Broadway hit honoring returning GIs, just as was done with *This Is the Army* and *Yip Yip, Yaphank* in previous wars. Lt. St. Pierre had somehow reached the producer's office of the Broadway production and received permission to do the show with the strong proviso from management (my father, king nepotism, had answered the call) that they get a professional person to direct it and, remarkably, there I was. Hence my transfer to New Jersey and my direction of the show, which toured most of the First Army bases and resulted in my ultimate stay at Dix as chief of Special Services for my required two-year stint.

Happily, I got out after two years, erasing my fear of being sent to Korea, and joined Biff who was involved in a new play by the great Sidney Kingsley entitled *Lunatics and Lovers*, then in auditions. Mr. Kingsley, known for *Dead End, Detective Story*, and *Darkness at Noon* was a stickler for routine, which he enjoyed, and which killed Biff and me. Thus, Biff, and I spent our days auditioning actors for the supporting roles and our nights assisting in rewrites, which Mr. Kingsley read to us in his den at his apartment in the Dakota. We had Buddy Hackett, a well-known comedian, in his first shot on Broadway, Sheila Bond and Dennis King, both veteran players and from Hollywood, the great Arthur O'Connell, Oscar-nominated for *Picnic,* and Mary Anderson, actress and wife of Leon Shamroy, Oscar-winning cinematographer of *Cleopatra, The King and I*, and other small films. Biff would stay out front with Mr. K and I would usher actors in and out, as they read pieces from a dummy script given to them. Biff would be as kind as possible when he delivered the haunting "NEXT!"

In the evenings the routine had you sounding out suggestions and reactions as Kingsley desired while he worked on revisions. A totally exhausting schedule. One night, claiming an oncoming cold, but needing sleep, Biff ran out of the Dakota as fast as he could. Later, Kingsley invited me to a little late supper at the Cafe des Artistes. I was dying to question him about the filming of *Dead End*, working with a young Bogart, and if he remembered Phil Adler from the Group Theatre days, so I joined him. At another table in the nearly empty restaurant sat Marilyn Monroe with her partner in a newly established production company, the photographer, Milton Greene. Greene probably told Marilyn who Kingsley was because she waved, and Kingsley moved right in. It was known that Marilyn was at odds with Los Angeles and so he chatted away about how fabulous the theater was, how exciting to work in front of a live audience and quick, wouldn't she love to do his new play? Her relationship with the playwright Arthur Miller never crossed his mind.

They schmoozed away at each other and fantasized how great it would be to conquer Broadway. I had a few fantasies myself, sitting there with The *Her,* and they had little to do with the American theater. Later, Greene invited us to his studio to show pictures he and Marilyn had just done in the Arizona desert. So, we all bundled ourselves in a taxi, an old one that had a jump seat one could pull out and sit on. Behold, there I was playing kneesies with Marilyn Monroe, staring into the most incredible blue eyes in history. Even her knees were gorgeous. At the studio the photos were gorgeous. Projected on his screen, the effect was gorgeous. The nudes were gorgeous. The whole adventure was gorgeous. She really was a life-time experience. Sidney promised to have the script delivered to her hotel in the morning, which he did, and we never heard from her again. I don't think she ever read it.

Anyway, the play was a minor hit, even without Ms. Monroe, running almost a year, and when it closed, a limited run on the West Coast was announced. I figured I could take advantage of an offer Leon Shamroy made and do a little networking in hopes of breaking into movies as an assistant director. So, I took over the road company as stage manager, O'Connell rented me an apartment on Malibu Beach, and off I went, anxious to break into the "movies." While we did recast Zero Mostel in the lead, the rest of the cast remained the same. *Lunatics and Lovers* was scheduled to play three cities before opening in Los Angeles. Zero was in some trouble getting work due to the blacklist which was hurting and even killing people suspected of having Communist leanings. It was obvious HUAC (House Un-American Activities Committee), the red-baiting, witch-hunting group was after Zero, attempting to subpoena him to testify and name names, which he would never do. To testify would probably have landed him in prison so it certainly was in his interest to "get out of Dodge." It would have been easy to serve him if he was housebound in New York and we made it extremely difficult to find him "on the road." With the help of our costume ladies, we would invent disguises that avoided detection. He was a porter, a stagehand, an usher, even a cleaning lady coming out of the stage door at night, walking past the servers waiting to nail him. Yes, he was the homeliest cleaning lady in the history of show business, but they never found him, and the show did big business and closed as scheduled in August of 1955. All that made the tour fun and exciting, and I ended up in my rented beach house facing the Pacific. It was a two-bedroom place with a deck that led down to the beach. The guy who owned it wanted to sell it to me for fourteen-thousand dollars, and I would have bought it too, but the networking was going badly around the studios. Shamroy was great to me, even inviting me to a party at his home where they showed a film after dinner. Naturally, I didn't know a soul and I found myself out on the terrace for a smoke.

There was a guy out there smoking a cigar, just the two of us, he finally tossed it off and stepped out of the shadows, offering his hand, and said, "Hi. Clark Gable. How are you?"

My first TOP JOB on Broadway. Photo courtesy of Playbill

2 | Rex Harrison. Dame Julie Andrews. Moss Hart. Alan J. Lerner. Former First Lady Jacqueline Kennedy. Former President John F. Kennedy.

The telegram from nepotism central read: "Doing musical *Pygmalion*. Get home quick. Dad."

Hoping Biff would be involved, I called him. It was true, he was involved, and Herman Levin was producing a musical based on Bernard Shaw's *Pygmalion*.

"What a terrible idea! They're going to sing and dance in Higgins's study?" I queried.

"They got Lerner and Loewe to do the score and Moss Hart to direct. Don't be so intelligent and get back here," said Biff.

If Moss Hart was involved, who was I to question the telegram? As soon as my lease expired, I sold my Studebaker and flew home, disregarding my fear of flying. There was a meeting at Herman Levin's office at 424 Madison Avenue as soon as I got back. Herman and Phil brought both Biff and me up to date on what was sealed at the time. It was a hell of a group. Moss Hart was, indeed, the director. Alan Jay Lerner was the lyricist and wrote the book; it was a project he had been mulling over ever since Harvard but couldn't solve. Frederick Loewe did the score. Oliver Smith, Levin's old partner, was on scenic design. Cecil Beaton, who wanted to do both sets and costumes, had finally agreed to concentrate on costumes. Hanya Holm was choreographer, and brought along Trude Rittman to do the dance arrangements. Franz Allers, Loewe's choice, was musical conductor and David Craig was on vocal arrangements. Finally, the extraordinary Robert Russell Bennett would do the orchestrations. Most of them were brought over from Lerner & Loewe's *Brigadoon*, a major hit on Broadway.

But all was not well: the musicalization of Shaw's play which had hounded Lerner for years was still hovering over the production. We were not privy to where the material was at present, and the office had not been supplied with a script. Mr. Levin had optioned Lerner's pitch and enthusiasm and, as a result, everyone was sailing along on the confidence and reliance that a fabulous resume can create. Everyone wanted Rex Harrison for the lead, and it took a small percentage (of the projected profits) to get the London management to release him from the play he was appearing in. Julie Andrews, a hit in *The Boy Friend*, and Stanley Holloway were also set.

Moss had left word that he and Alan Lerner were holing up in Atlantic City and wouldn't return until they could produce a working script. It sounded to me like Orson Welles again vowing never to appear unless . . . But, by God, two weeks later they appeared, and we had a script. In fact, with the exception of a scene called "Dressing Eliza for the Ball," which was eventually cut in Philadelphia, it was really the final script.

Auditions went fast and well; the staff knew what they wanted. We had rented the roof of the New Amsterdam movie theater that had been the scene of the Ziegfeld Midnight Frolic. It was perfect because it had two large rooms offstage for the dancing and singing rehearsals. The main auditorium was decrepit and filthy, as it had been abandoned for over thirty years. We had it cleaned up, searched for rats, and repaired by the time we were ready. While it's well-known by now that there's no sense listing the cast, it gave one a stir to see them all together that December day in 1955.

Everything was ready: we had a script, a great cast, and the rehearsal space was livable. Biff and I had marked the acting areas on the stage floor according to Oliver's floor plans, and we had just received our first payroll check. It was signed by The Liza Company and offered a vivid reminder: what's the name of the show? Many suggestions had been made: "London Dock," "Fair Eliza," "Our Song," all terrible, until Bob Adams, Herman Levin's office manager, walked into the final production meeting humming, "London Bridge is Falling Down," and we all sang out "MY FAIR LADY."

It went swimmingly for a while; Rex insisting more of Shaw be used as dialogue (he carried a beat-up Penguin paper edition of the play in his back pocket) and Julie, a little awed by the proceedings, as if she was out of place. Moss and Lerner acquiesced a bit to Rex's suggestions and Moss took Julie by the hand. On our first cast day off, Biff and I, playing everyone, went scene by scene quietly encouraging her to realize she was really the core of the play and the star of the musical. A tremendous psychological performance by Mr. Hart and a rejuvenation for Julie.

The smell was in the air. When you're involved in exquisite material flawlessly put together, there is that mysterious air that covers everything. By the end of the first run-through, it was there. With the exception of Murphy's Law (if anything can possibly go wrong, it will), we had a hit on our hands. The only question was, how big?

We completed run-throughs every afternoon, so by the time we were to leave town for the New Haven, Connecticut break-in, the cast was fully prepared for our first performance with an audience. The Shubert Theatre was a famous try-out place but a terribly tiny one. The load-in and put-up took an inordinate length of time due to stage dimensions and delays of delivery in snowstorms that hit every day. The cast arrived on that Wednesday before our Saturday preview. They rehearsed with the orchestra at the Jewish Community Center up the street while the crew crammed the scenery onto the stage. *My Fair Lady* was a double turntable show and prior to digital mechanics, the tables were controlled by cable and winch.

Murphy's Law was rampant—nothing fit, everything was a problem that took time so that by Saturday, not Friday as initially planned, we called the first dress rehearsal. As for the afternoon before our first preview, there aren't enough reams of paper to describe the obstacles that initial day. Did we put the change up costumes in the right place? Are the props in their proper area? Are the lights focused properly? And, oh Lord, do the turntables turn and stop correctly without sending the scenery into the orchestra pit? Speaking of the orchestra pit, Rex hadn't gotten over the shock of a huge orchestra joining him every time he started to sing. He had only recently tolerated the piano accompaniment on the New Amsterdam roof. We started fitfully, and by the time we revolved into Higgins's study we had taken an enormous bite out of the allotted schedule, anxious minutes we couldn't afford to waste.

We began "I'm An Ordinary Man," and Rex suddenly stopped and said, "Mossy, Mossy, if you're out there . . ."

A beleaguered Moss Hart faintly called back, "Yes, Rex."

Rex strolled to the apron of the stage and said, "You may as well know it now as later. I will not open in this play tonight. As a matter of fact, I may never open in it. Get yourself another boy!"

At that moment, everything seemed insurmountable to him,

and he left the stage. Moss told the nervous cast to continue the dress rehearsal with Rex's standby as Higgins. With that, he and Alan Jay went into Rex's dressing room. We hadn't signed a Rex standby, but we limped along with Biff starring as Higgins. There was a big racket coming out of that room, it was getting late, and we were going nowhere. Later, Moss emerged and announced a break, there was to be no performance and we should meet at the Jewish Center at 9 p.m. A forlorn group quickly left the scene of the crime and Biff, me, and the crew ran the cues, with one eye glued to the dressing room door. In the midst of this commotion, Morris Bailey, the theater owner came storming down the aisle.

He grabbed Phil Adler, who was guarding Rex's dressing room door, screaming, "Phil, Phil, you've got to play tonight. What do you mean no preview? They're coming from all over in this snowstorm! They'll tear me limb from limb! I beg you!"

Phil quickly calmed him. "Morris, don't you worry, we'll open tonight. If you can play Higgins, we're all set."

A parade of lawyers, agents, and producers filled Rex's room and the real result of Rex's interrogation is not known, only that Moss emerged from the room a little before six and victoriously announced, "Gather the players. We open tonight!"

Gather the players? Is he kidding? Where will we find everyone a mere two hours away from curtain time? With the horror of total cancellation in the air, they must all be in hibernation feeling the worst. We combed the town, we got the staff from the hotel to bang on doors, we announced the news at both nearby restaurants. We stopped the movie downtown and made the call to "Get to the Shubert!" Miraculously we found everyone except Rosemary Gaines, one of the singers, who, we found out later, was having appendix surgery at that very moment.

The creeping dread that we had never done the whole show with cast, scenery, costumes, and props made no difference, we were troupers, and we were bent on performing. The sodden, snow-drenched theatergoers were on their way, the cast was in costume and, as a final touch, Moss felt a word of warning was due the audience. He stepped out in front of the house curtain and gave one of the great psychological warm-ups of all time:

"Because of terrible technical difficulties and the complexities of the production we felt we could not do our play as you would want," he announced, as groans from the audience filled the theater. "Much thought was given to postponing tonight," he continued, as the audience, sitting in pools of melting snow, heaved a collective sigh. "In spite of our difficulties, and because we knew you had braved the elements, you would want us to play tonight." At this, the audience roared with delight. "Tonight, we will give our first performance. To quote one of my favorite plays, 'we depend upon the kindness of strangers.'" We could have sung the phone book and been a hit after that tearjerker.

Rex turned out to be a tower of strength that night. Julie, relieved that he was banging along, did her best. Due to endless stage waits forced on us by unmanageable scenic disasters, Higgins's study kept rolling into the wings every time we tried a revolve. The audience couldn't care less, sitting there, warming up and drying out, they applauded every moment, cheered at intermission and thanks to Lerner's script, there was only one revolve in the second act. Some three hours later, bent but not broken, we slowly put the study in place for the last scene behind the street curtain while Rex was singing "I've Grown Accustomed to Her Face." The song ended, the reaction out front was enormous, and the lights faded out on cue. Rex was supposed to come down from the house set he had been singing on, but there was no Rex in sight, only total darkness. Where the hell was he? We were in uncharted territory.

From the wings, I could barely see Rex standing there on the unit staring out into limbo as if he was counting the house. Flashlight in hand, I came around, opened the door of the set and grabbed Rex's arm.

"Christ, where am I?" He said, blinking into the darkness.

"It's okay, it's Jerry," I said.

We had never rehearsed this.

"Who?" Rex asked.

"Never mind, I'll help you down," I said, as I took a firm grip on him.

"My God, is it all over?" He hoped.

"One more scene with Julie," I said, as I brought him down.

"Take me . . . *somewhere*," he requested, and I got him into the study for the finale.

The reception at the final curtain was ecstatic, the place shook with applause. Were we that good? We must have been. The whole aura of confidence built up since rehearsals at the New Amsterdam roof slowly came back. By Monday we were back at positive strength. The official opening went beautifully; the audience reaction, if nothing else, was amazing. We were a genuine smash!

One of the fabulous things about the Biz is courage. We roll the dice with everything on the line more often than any fanatic gambler ever does. Career, unemployment, security, fame—whatever it all means, we dare to do it. So, who can blame our eccentricities? Working with that kind of pressure and liking it! That's the kind of marvelous satisfaction this business gives. The more you gamble, the bigger the odds—the greater the exultation at the instant of success.

The week's stay in New Haven ended with the production running smoothly. Even with all the technical issues solved, the performance evolved as Moss cleaned any glitches remaining from the hazards of the opening days. We finished the final performance that Saturday and, just as the takeout had begun—the audience was gone, the cast was back at the hotel packing up for our trip to Philadelphia, the crew was beginning the break-down of the production and load-out to the trucks—I thought I heard something out front. I was the last of the cast to leave, cleaning up the stage manager's desk and disconnecting the cue board. We hadn't taken props out the front doors yet, so it was curious to hear anything out there. I left the wings and stood stage center, listening. It was a murmur and a little voice moaning, coming from my left down near the box seats. It was disturbing, so I went through the passageway and found a woman lying near the wall of seats.

She was murmuring, "Oh my God, oh my God."

I quickly asked if I could help, if I should call for an ambulance, and where she was experiencing pain.

To my surprise, she said, "Oh, my god. The baby's coming!"

I said a few "Oh my Gods," too.

"Can I help you? Can I call a doctor? What . . ." I asked.

"Wait. My husband went for the car. Oh, God, just wait."

With that I took off my jacket and rolled it up under her head.

She thanked me and shrieked, "It's coming, oh God, open my coat, I . . ."

I opened her coat and the baby fell out of her body, wrapped in her underwear. She cried out, and not knowing what the hell to do, I grabbed my jacket, lifted the slippery thing, and warmed it in my coat. Just then, the husband came running in from the open fire door. He took one look at what was going on and I think he leaked in his pants. In total silence they gathered everything up and staggered out the door. I stood there in amazement until the prop guys started coming out with their first load. Then, it dawned on me: the son of a bitch stole my coat! That baby is now about sixty-five, and ready for Social

Security. I hope his parents told him the story of his birth and if they did, and he or she can think of it, can you give me back my jacket?

One of the nightmares stage managers go through is standing alone out there telling the audience that whomever they came to see, and paid good money to boot, will not appear. Case in point, back at *My Fair Lady* during the New York run, Julie Andrews got sick and couldn't perform. The audience was grim and disinterested in the fact that her understudy, Lola Fisher, was quite wonderful in the part. Soon all was well, the show was fine, and the audience, informed about Julie in advance, enjoyed the production. But by the middle of the second month Rex decided he had the flu and wanted to recover in Bermuda for a rest. As the stage manager, one must go out there and break the news to an eager audience after which they'll probably throw programs at you—and they actually did when Biff heroically did just that.

All understudies are well-rehearsed under good management. Tom Helmore, Rex's standby, felt ready, however, he insisted on a full orchestra rehearsal and a company rehearsal as well. Amazingly, Phil Adler, who hated spending company money, agreed. Tom was scheduled to play Friday night and two on Saturday while Rex was lolling in the Bermuda sun. Murphy's Law made a notable entrance and, by Friday night, Tom was feeling a raspy throat from all that rehearsal he had insisted upon. He had no great feeling of warmth from out front, instead they were hostile and insisting on refunds. We called the house doctor in, and he worked on Tom that night right there in the dressing room after the performance. Tom signed in little late for the Saturday matinee sounding like a crocodile in heat. We got the doctor back in, and he worked on Tom. What could we do? We were in standby-hell. What kind of hideous performance could he give? Whatever it was to be, it's all we had. And what about Julie, who turned a little ashen when she heard the news about Tom? She didn't want both leads out at the same time, but she had been nursing a cold all week and, to her credit, never complained. We checked on Dr. Epiglottis who was jamming awful things down poor Tom's throat during half hour, all to no avail. It all seemed hopeless. Biff pleaded with Phil for a cancellation: how could we go on in light of the misery backstage and the poor quality of performance?

"I don't give back the money. It's tough enough to get it. I don't give it back," answered Phil.

With obvious trepidation, we began. It was dreadful, the sounds coming out of Tom's mouth were hideous. By the first break, while Doolittle was on, the mad physician was wielding his silver roto rooter, ably spraying, and excavating globs of phlegm from poor Tom's larynx. Not quite over her own illness, Julie was showing evidence of laryngitis. Even Phil agreed, "the only ones left are the ushers."

We pulled the curtain, and pandemonium broke out at the box office. The audience was given refunds on their eight-dollar tickets, for which most of them had paid ten times as much, or more. It took the police to clear the lobby. Peace was eventually restored. Rex, previously warned, came back for the evening show, and poor Tom went home.

During the late days of *My Fair Lady*, Moss saw the show a couple of times and gave notes to the company. One such day, he invited Biff and me to accompany him to see a preview of a new show directed by Bretaigne Windust (his real name, I swear) that Sunday in Dover, Delaware. Biff could not go and Moss's wife, Kitty Carlisle, was doing a TV show that night. The chance to spend some interesting time with Moss alone was tantalizing, and I accepted the offer.

It was a long drive, almost three hours, but he had agreed to give his opinion on the merits of the play. He did these things quite often being one of the theater's greats. While Dover was a little farther than he should have been asked to go, the trip was terrific; Moss told some anecdotes, we shared a packed lunch, the limo was comfortable, and Moss was able to nap for a bit.

We arrived just in time, and the management greeted him like visiting royalty, which he loved. They sat us down on the aisle and before we could read the program, the house lights dimmed, and the curtain rose on a beautiful set. A kind of baronial living room, it had a staircase on our left reminiscent of the one in Higgins's study. The audience applauded the lavish scenery, and at the curve of the staircase, a green glow grew brighter and brighter. Moss tapped me on the shoulder and said, "Leprechaun." And so it was, from over on our right there came David Wayne, dressed in full leprechaun regalia, just as he had worn in *Finian's Rainbow* (his huge hit performance), hanging on an invisible wire so as to appear to be flying. We all applauded as he soared across the stage heading for the green glow on the staircase. It was quite marvelous as he flew, but due to Murphy's Law, he missed the steps and BANG! He tore a gaping hole in the wall as he crashed through it and disappeared.

The audience stopped their applause and gasped at the accident. You could hear the commotion and cursing as stagehands tried to catch him. Here he came out of the green glow, now flying backwards and flailing his arms and legs in the air. There were a few giggles as he flew off into the area he came from. More screaming, cursing, and commotion erupted from the dark off stage but to no avail. Momentum brought him into view, a little slower now, his costume showing the wear and tear the crew had made trying to catch him. His hat was gone, one sleeve had been partially torn away, his face was terribly pale, and a curly little green shoe fell off as he headed back to the green void he had created. By now the applause and laughter had turned into a riot as he disappeared and quickly reappeared to great celebration. But it wasn't appreciated by Mr. Wayne as he finally came to a tottering stop, dead center stage, looking like they had hung the hapless leprechaun in public. The curtain began slowly falling, and the last thing we saw during the bedlam around us was the little green shoe on the leprechaun's foot, pawing the air.

In the middle of all the chaos and noise, Moss turned to me and said, "Funny play! A little short, but really funny."

We snuck out before anyone could find us and we roared all the way back to New York. Moss especially liked my rendition of a leprechaun flying backward. The memory of this is tainted by the fact that I never saw Moss Hart again. A few weeks later he had a heart attack at his vacation home in Palm Springs and died on the lawn as Kitty was getting the car out to take him to the dentist. He was fifty-seven years old.

In early 1960, there were discussions between the State Department, the Liza Company, the American National Theatre and Academy (ANTA, now a relic), and Goskoncert, then the cultural organization of the Soviet Union. The outcome of the talks, originally sponsored by Mamie Eisenhower, Jackie Kennedy (soon to be First Lady), and Mr. Khrushchev was a cultural exchange program. The Bolshoi Ballet would come to America and *My Fair Lady* would be the first theatrical production to be seen in Russia since *Porgy and Bess* which played there many years ago. The financial arrangements were agreed upon, and the State Department would cover expenses on our part, and both countries would enjoy any profits the performances would incur within their respective borders. The Liza Company would be reimbursed for any expenses, all they would supply was technical advice as to acceptable facilities in each city proposed. The final results, based on our recommendations, would be decided after a technical investigation was done. Biff and I were sent in advance to establish which theater and in what city *My Fair Lady* could play, as well as to finalize drawings of the scenery to be constructed in the Soviet Union. The Russians wanted six cities and four performances in each, and Herman Levin was pushing us to agree to four cities and get back as soon as possible. We flew first class to Paris, and they put us up at the Ritz! We were to meet a European entrepreneur the State Department hired as an advisor and translator. Anatole Heller would prove to be useful and quickly advised us that we had been ordered by President Eisenhower to make sure the project happened. With Ike involved, the whole project took on some heavy pressure.

To get to Moscow, we flew on what looked like a DC-3 (this is long before Aeroflot), which had a tangle of oxygen tubes hanging over each seat. There was no food, no drinks, and no other passengers. On landing in Moscow, we were greeted by a group in furry hats and long sleeves. We learned later that long sleeves were used instead of gloves. Smart, because it was cold, I mean cold. All hotels in Russia at that time were built to look like they had always been there. We were put up at the Hotel Ukraina. Huge rooms with nothing in them except a bed, a chair, and a radio. Everything was a little seedy: the bathrooms were a sinister joke. Mine had no tub, just an overhead shower head next to a small chandelier. The idea was to empty the room and take a shower. The drain was on the floor next to the sink, which had a tiny orange disk with a name on it, *Sop*. I guess *Sop* was a government issue because everyone smelled from that sweet, sickly odor. Forget about toilet paper—they supplied what felt like thin sheets of cardboard. Thank God I brought plenty of Kleenex as Mr. Heller had recommended.

The Red Army Theater in Moscow, also called the Stanislavski, was used by the army to display tanks and the stage was as big as a football field. It was amazing that in most of the cities we visited, there stood an extraordinary theater. Even in rather small and slightly rundown towns, there stood their theater. At the Red Army Theater, we took on a group of stage technicians that would follow us as we visited each city. They were the guys who would construct the physical production and prepare each take-in. They took notes as we inspected the stages. It was fabulous to see how much one could get done using simple sign language. The fly floor was adequate with plenty of hemp lying around, and it was agreed that a proscenium would be built to frame the theater's stage since the width of the wings were huge. All in all, it was a great meeting and Moscow would be the first city where *My Fair Lady* would play. There was a day off and we tried to get into the Stalin-Lenin mausoleum, but the line was around the block. We dashed across the road from the Kremlin and jumped into the GUM Department store, mainly to warm up. Michael Petrovski was our guide, and we eventually were ushered into The Bolshoi Ballet Theatre to enjoy a performance.

We were then onto Leningrad on the Red Arrow Express, a train which was expressly built by the Czar to run as straight and narrow as an arrow flew—no bumps, no curves. I shared a cozy compartment with lamps, a table, and carpeting. It was quite lovely. The only catch was the fact that Biff and I shared the coziness with another traveler, a huge Siberian gentleman in need of a shave. Biff had the lower bunk, I had the upper, and there he was. What does one do while sharing a bedroom with strangers? I smiled a lot, so did Biff, and there were stares all around. Who gets undressed first? I'm sure not getting naked with the Siberian in the room, so who uses the tiny toilet first . . . or at all? Finally, Biff suggested we retire to the bar car while our tenant attended to his toilette. The bar was a fine idea, as the stagehands were there and after many vodka and lemon peels, I could have slept with a Russian bear.

The Worker's Theater in Leningrad was almost equal in size and equipment, so we had a little time to visit the Hermitage, an aging museum that used to be the Czar's summer palace. The way everybody else in the city lived, no wonder they revolted. We had a full day in Leningrad, which turned out to be the most beautiful city in the country.

The trip to Minsk was downright frightening. It was our first plane ride inside the Soviet Union and, of course, there was a dilapidated DC3 waiting for us. Most of these passengers had waited many hours for this flight since there didn't seem to be a schedule. When a flight you wanted came up, you left the spot you had been camping in and jumped aboard. We were lucky, having a VIP pass. The most dangerous thing was the take-off. No sooner had everyone boarded the plane when it started down the runway with no hostess and plenty of scramblers. It took off with most of the people wandering around looking for seats. As we neared our destination, we experienced the same routine: everybody got up, grabbed their coats, and had conversations as we landed. Unbelievable.

Minsk turned out to be a tiny, distressed city caught in the agricultural problems that plagued the "breadbasket" of the Ukraine. Yet there it was, in the middle of slums and depression, a wonderful theater, quite a testament to the cultural life these Belarusians hung onto. The hotel was a lot like the others; this lobby, however, was totally empty except for the sign-in desk. The rooms were huge and equally empty. The whole place was really dismal. Yet it turned out to be the most exciting time of our entire trip. We went directly to the theater and met our Belarusian crew. Biff and I had learned a few important stage terms in Russian and, together with some really eager pantomime, we acted out the entire show for the men, who were following with floor plans and enjoying the performance. There came to be a comradeship and intimacy with these guys I had never experienced with strangers, all of us utilizing our imagination and craft in an exchange of knowledge. Unfortunately, by the end of our time together, it was apparent that the Minsk Theatre could never accommodate the show and Michael Petrovski, who was the gaffer of the group, notified Goskoncert that Minsk was out of the question. This probably pleased the State Department that two of the cities would probably be canceled.

The flight to Odessa was much of the same routine, passengers standing when they should be sitting and vice versa. There was only one unusual thing that came to my attention as we were circling over farm country and descending:

"So, Biff, we're crash landing, right?" I queried, as I, surprisingly calmly, considered how I'd probably come all this way just to be sent home in a box.

All kidding aside, we were coming in fast and THUD! We hit and bounced a mile. The unfazed Ukrainians behind us were used to this maneuver and were already hanging onto seat backs and door-knobs. After coming to a rest on the ground, the engine started roaring. We slowly headed through the marsh to a one-story building: Odessa! After several attempts to climb onto the concrete walkway, the last try being a huge success, we banged into the terminal wall. Odessa by the Red Sea! Wow. I once had visions of Hedy Lamar smoking on my balcony, viewing the tranquil waters below. Forget about it! The Red Sea below my balcony was full of oil derricks, the kind you see in Los Angeles on your way to the airport. It took no time to realize that this city and nearby Tiflis were miles from Moscow. And, according to Goskoncert, it was intended to transfer the production by rail, which would have eaten up most of the time we were to play in the Soviet Union. Goskoncert unhappily agreed, as did Tom Tuck, the State Department liaison in Moscow. Additionally, the theater was too small and mildly under equipped. It was finally agreed that Moscow,

Leningrad and, if possible, Kiev would be where *My Fair Lady* would play.

Kiev was perfect, a lovely theater and the best equipped backstage we had encountered in the country. Interestingly, across the street from the front of the house, there was a large furniture store with windows displaying their goods in little vignettes. One was a dining room with a table surrounded with family and kids playing on the floor. The one that struck me was of a living room, with mom and pop on a couch alongside their kid. Behind them was a maid in full regalia: a black woman dressed as a maid. I hadn't seen a person of color in all the time I was here in Russia, they must have gotten the idea from Hollywood. Now that the itinerary was set, we were told to be ready to leave the hotel within the hour, not even enough time to say a farewell to our terrific crew. We were hustled by plane to Moscow, to a waiting Air France jet, and were set to return home having done a perfect job. Sitting there, drink in hand, we were told to buckle up, but having recently assimilated to the Soviet style of air travel, we refrained.

In the States, arrangements had quickly begun. The Chicago company would be sent with Edward Mulhare and Lola Fisher from the New York production while Michael Allinson and Anne Rogers from Chicago would play New York. Michael Petrovski sent word the turntables were done and installed, and everything was ready to go. Off they flew, one plane with cast and orchestrations, one cargo plane with some scenery, props, and costumes. I didn't go, as I had to keep the Hellinger Theatre going, but Biff was sent to produce the event. My folks went, Phil as company manager and Polly Adler, my mother as a tourist. The reports of the Moscow opening were rapturous. As proof, there is a picture of that night showing the audience as the curtain fell. In the entire theater, there was one person giving a standing ovation: my mother! In Russia, the audience never stands, applauding but remaining seated. Later, as the cast was set to move on to Leningrad, there was news that an American U-2 reconnaissance plane had been shot down over Russia. The American pilot, Gary Powers, had been captured and all the built-up relationships and cordial hand-shakings we had enjoyed were dead. The production was immediately ordered to pack up and get out. All the work and all the cooperation were for naught. The show was "to get out of town before it was too late," and that was that.

Shortly after the stench of the Russian disaster had died down, I got a call from the office that Alan Lerner was bringing the reigning First Lady, Jackie Kennedy, to that day's matinee. President Kennedy had recently succeeded President Eisenhower and the Kennedy's were a hot couple. Most arrangements for her attendance were problems for the front of house, I just had to wait for a sign that she was in and seated before we started the performance. I informed Rex, and Julie, as well as the company that they should remain onstage to greet Mrs. Kennedy. The only nuisance was, as the overture began, the appearance of a few Secret Service agents backstage. I assured the head guy that there were no assassins in the cast, but they hovered in the wings anyway. In retrospect, my use of the word "assassin" is awful.

Jackie received an ovation when she appeared with Lerner and the performance settled down quite soon. About twenty minutes later, the head Secret Service agent, who had been talking into his wrist, took me aside and informed me that the president had changed his schedule and was now joining his wife at the theater, and could I show the group how to get President Kennedy into the theater without bringing him through the front of the house. I suggested bringing him in back, through the loading dock, and escorting him backstage to the passage door into the auditorium. The Secret

Service troupe agreed, and the head guy talked into his wrist setting up the deal. Rex Partington had been running the cues, as Biff had left for another show, so I informed Rex about the situation. I then took the agent out back to show him the side street and the alleyway to the dock. As the entourage neared the alley, they told me to wait on the dock and greet the president of the United States, for God's sake, and escort him and the men to the passage door. I stood there, quite nervously, tentatively waiting to meet him; a man I greatly admired. As perspiration began to show my trepidations, I contemplated, *what I should say? Do I shake his hand? How do I greet him? Should I tell him who I am? Why would he care? Should I . . . ?* I see the caravan approaching. He doesn't ride alone, look at the line of limos. *Oh, my god, he's getting out of the car! He really looks like him.* I'm nervous, you know, this is a big deal for me. *Lord, he's getting close, jeez he's some good-looking guy.* He's up the steps, heading right for me. *What do I say?* He's putting out his hand.

I grabbed his hand, shook it, and blurted out, "Good afternoon, I am the president of the United States." Laughs all around.

He saw the mountain of eggs on my face and put a hand on my shoulder and said, "Well, that makes two of us."

Grins and laughs again, including me. I took him to the passage door, and he snuck his way to sit with his wife.

Original Playbill from My Fair Lady. *Photo courtesy of Playbill*

Teaching Eliza her lessons in My Fair Lady

The opening of My Fair Lady. *One woman standing, my mother*

3 | Barbra Streisand. Jack Benny. Sir Noël Coward. José Ferrer. Florence Henderson. Jerry Herman. Hal Holbrook. Elliott Gould. Lesley Ann Warren. Mike Nichols. Barbara Harris. Alan Alda.

The show Biff had gone off to do was *Bravo, Giovanni* and he asked me to help him with principal auditions. I didn't need the money right then, so I did it for Biff who stayed out front with the higher-ups while I funneled the prospective artists in and out. They had rented one of the Shubert Theaters and the auditions were held on a blank stage with a piano. They already had Cesare Siepi, an Italian Basso Opera star, and Michelle Lee, a well-known soubrette. I had no idea what the show was about or what they needed, but they kept auditioning for days. One day, in walked a young woman dressed in what I would call Greenwich Village gypsy. She opened her guitar case and waited. Brenda Vaccaro sang just before her, and I waited for "NEXT!" before I announced the next one. While we stood there in the wings, she handed me her resume and asked if I could let her use my stool. I brought her stool and resume out front, gave it to Biff, and announced:

"Barbara Streisand, no piano."

She came out and sat, ignoring the usual fuss and noise from the front. She started to sing, and I nearly had chills. I had done a million auditions, but I never heard anything so soft and clear, warm, and mesmerizing. She sang "Smile," the old Charlie Chaplin song, and quieted the whole theater. Even the cleaning lady up in the balcony sat and listened. I was absolutely possessed, not wanting her to stop. But finally, she did.

She dragged my stool and her guitar over to me and said, "Thanks, but it's Barbra, two a's not three," and left.

I thought I'd hear what I expected to hear, "*huzzah*!" Instead, there was an argument going on. I didn't want to intrude, but the line I did hear came from Stanley Prager, the director of the show:

"Yeah, she's really something. But did you get a shot of her nose? Come on, that's one homely lady."

Brenda Vaccaro got the part. The show lasted five months. Barbra did better.

My Fair Lady closed in September of 1962 and *Moby Dick—Rehearsed* followed in December, leaving me at liberty as the old saying goes. I visited the Levin office as part of a networking drill and found out Herman was in preparation to produce *The Girl Who Came to Supper*, a musical version of the popular film *The Prince and the Showgirl,* starring Laurence Olivier and Marilyn Monroe. Naturally the idea was to get the two of them to do the musical. Good luck.

But as my good luck would have it, an old gin-rummy pal of my father's, Irving Fein, contacted me. He was producing, along with the Theatre Guild, an evening with Jack Benny, the great radio and television comedian, at my old haunt, the Ziegfeld Theatre. It certainly sounded like a strange trio: a staid old theater organization dedicated to presenting fine drama, a minor producer, and one of the most universally loved performers who hadn't been on Broadway in many years. The job was to meet Mr. Benny in Toronto where he had just received some honorary award, bring him and his group to the city, and drop him off at the Warwick Hotel up the street from the Ziegfeld. The greeting I got from him was so friendly, I loved him instantly. He seemed so eager to do the show. All of us—Jack, his musical conductor Maylon Merrick, and Mr. Merrick's wife— flew to New York that day. He seemed a trifle frail and hesitant. Walking to the hotel, I began worrying about his stamina doing eight shows a week, but was informed by Mr. Fein, an old friend of Jack's, that he'd be fine.

The Guild had hired a veteran designer, Sam Leve, and when I got to the theater everything was in order, lighting, drapery, and curtains. I sure came on late. The show was simple; there was a singing group, and Jane Morgan, a well-known cabaret singer, to do the first half of the program then, after intermission, Jack Benny was on. All we had to do was bring him to the wings and, at the proper moment, tap him on his shoulder, and he would take over and entertain the audience for at least an hour.

Opening night went great; the first act was very entertaining and after the intermission it was Jack's turn. I came to his dressing room and found him sitting quietly on the couch. On a signal, he rose very achingly and lost a little balance, but he took my arm, and we went to the stage. *Can this man make it? Can he do an hour of stand-up? Are we in deep trouble here?* He was only in his seventies, but he sure seemed older than that. He leaned against my prom desk and waited. On my cue, the house lights dimmed, the stage lights brightened, and I tapped him on his shoulder—you had to be there, it was like the painting on the Sistine Chapel ceiling where God's finger ignites life! I tapped him and he suddenly lost thirty years, straightened, and purposely strode onto the stage. It was a little weird and absolutely amazing, but there he was, the Jack Benny we all knew, killing the people.

I had one other cue: the violin bit. Jack would tell everyone that he was actually a concert violinist, and, in fact, plays on a very rare Stradivarius violin. He would then ask the audience if they would like to hear him play and, after much applause, he would call to me in the wings to bring out his very expensive violin. After a beat, I threw out a violin that crash landed at his feet. It landed with shattered pieces of violin flying all over and the audience collapsed. Jack just stood there, hands crossed, staring at me. The longer he stared, the longer they laughed. It happened every night of that happy run at the Ziegfeld. When it ended, he gave me a hug and slipped a box into my jacket. It was a Tiffany box containing a gold money clip with my initials in Old English etched on the front and his signature on the back. Imagine, the guy touted to be the world's most famous miser giving me gold.

By now, Herman Levin had put together a formidable group: Noël Coward, music and lyrics; Joe Layton, director and choreographer; and a top production staff including Oliver Smith, Irene Shataff, and Jay Blackton. He couldn't land Olivier or Marilyn Monroe, but he blessed us with two big Broadway talents: José Ferrer and Florence Henderson. We also signed Tessie O'Shea, a terrific cockney character. Of course, I was set. Auditions went well, everything in rehearsals went well, and we had a wonderfully talented and professional cast, so off we went to Boston for a pre-Broadway tryout. However, there was one little hitch: wireless microphones had just come to Broadway and every performer in musicals wanted one. They were cumbersome items you carried on your body, tied by a slender wire to a microphone buried in your hair—a pain in the ass most of the time. The problem with Mr. Ferrer was his genitals. The sound guy wanted to bury the transmitter box somewhere near Mr.

Ferrer's crotch but since he was so well endowed, they settled on taping it to the small of his back. All of this was important because he was playing the role of the prince mainly in tights. Crisis averted, everyone was delighted, and the costume ladies named him "Hose."

We were on our pre-Broadway run in Philadelphia and were invited to a concert by the Philadelphia Symphony on our rare Friday afternoon off. In the middle of the performance, a man came on the stage interrupting the concert and whispering something to Eugene Ormandy. His anger that they had him stop the performance quickly turned to grief as he informed us that President Kennedy had been shot at a parade in Dallas. He had no other information but asked if we would stand while the orchestra played "The National Anthem." Most sang softly, and you could hear the sobs throughout the house. Our management announced cancellations of performances until further notice. We all hunkered down in hotel rooms and watched the footage of Jack Ruby killing Lee Harvey Oswald. By Monday, it was decided to resume performances after the president's funeral. These were the days before iPhones, laptops, and social media, so I was in the same dilemma as in New Haven: gather the players! I made more phone calls and hung more notices in hotel lobbies and on backstage bulletin boards that day than ever before. In a general malaise, just like the rest of the heartbroken nation, we all returned, dragged our asses backstage, and, I will not use the hackneyed phrase, we did get it done.

The show was good, the reviews both in Boston and New York were favorable. We had lavish costumes, a beautiful production, and first-rate leads which demonstrated the importance of material. So we settled in for a successful run. Before he had to return to the UK, Mr. Coward made many hilarious and sometimes wondrous remarks about José's privates. He even badgered Joe Layton, the director, to set up a note session with Ferrer in his dressing room in hopes of catching him undressed. Layton got Jose to play along, and we arranged it. Rumors and gags had been floating around backstage, mostly started by the costume department. On that particular night after the show, I escorted Noël and Layton to José's room supposedly to give notes. Jose was notified in advance that they were coming. I had no idea what Ferrer was up to.

I knocked on his door, and José yelled, "Come on in!"

We entered, and there he was, stark naked, bending over his sink, his face full of shaving cream. His penis was drifting in the soapy water, the head of which was hanging out over the edge of the sink. It was a remarkable and convincing sight, and the effect was not lost on any of us, especially not Noël, who had eagerly followed us in.

Joe gave a couple of silly notes as José finished shaving then turned to Noël and said, "I hear you're leaving. I'll miss you, old cock."

With a touch of jealousy, Noël responded, "Not so old, yes. Not so old."

We all enjoyed the ruse, laughing, and hugging Noël. It turned out to be the last we ever saw of that brilliant fellow, Noël Coward.

I was having quite an interesting time doing a few hits, including *Oh! What a Lovely War*, a very avant-garde musical produced by the British Theatre Workshop and directed by the ingenious Joan Littlewood. It was the only time I ever worked for David Merrick, thank heavens. His reputation as a tight-fisted son of a bitch preceded him although I never once laid eyes on him during the run. Actor's Equity insisted we include some American performers in the cast, so we eventually hired Brian Murray, Jack Edelman, and Reid Shelton who would go on to play the lead in *Annie*. The whole production was an improvisation on the insanity of war; Ms. Littlewood wanted the audience to leave the theater laughing at war. She had the actors in Pierrot costumes because she hated uniforms. The actors had no set script. I was given three lighting set-ups to call instinctively, and Joan shuffled the cast each night to encourage the individuality of the group. The whole experience kept me on my feet as we ran the projected four months.

An old friend of mine, Hal Holbrook, invited me to join him on a college tour he had booked doing his solo performance of *Mark Twain, Tonight*, his extraordinary impersonation of the legendary author. The basic idea, of course, was to bring it to Broadway if the material merited it. The material merited it, and hopefully it would enjoy a nice run. His one-man performance was the product of years of research and the hours it took to evoke Twain. The result was a marvel of detail. It literally took him over two hours of preparation to bring the old man to life. The show did come to Broadway and played four months after wonderful reviews.

Not having learned much from the past, I tried my hand as a producer by doing *Drat! The Cat!* A musical by Ira Levin and Paul Schafer. Together with Ira, an old friend and neighbor, we pitched the material to an aspiring and daring guy named Norman Rosemont who had offices in the Plaza Hotel. Norman loved it as did Joe Layton (to direct and choreograph). I loved having an office in the Plaza, suit and tie every day, feeling like a producer. The capitalization was raised by hook and real crook and so we went into production. Auditions were done quickly, and we cast Lesley Ann Warren as the female cat burglar and Elliott Gould as the policeman who chases, and eventually falls for her. Charles Durning, in his first job on Broadway, played the police chief. We all loved the show. Barbra Streisand, by now a major star and married to Elliott, recorded "He Touched Me," a hit song from the musical. It was a coup and helped our publicity substantially. Everything was rolling along, full-house previews went well. The show played fourteen previews and by opening night, Rosemont was smoking cigars. The critics panned the show and we closed in a week—even Barbra couldn't save us. Will I never learn?

I think Alexander H. Cohen, one of our great showmen of his time, hired me because I was working for David Merrick and he loved stealing from him. Mr. Cohen was doing *A Time for Singing* taken from Richard Llewellyn's great book, *How Green Was My Valley*. The musical, already in previews in Boston, needed some backstage reorganizing so Mr. Cohen hired me. I invented the term "Production Supervisor," and got all the problems worked out before we arrived in New York. The score by Gerald Freedman and John Morris was lovely and the singing terrific, but luck was not on our side. The show opened during a newspaper strike and the only critic to print a review was Stanley Kaufmann and his notice was so egregious and personally destructive to cast members that the *New York Times* fired him and hired Walter Kerr. Alas, it was too late to save our show which closed after forty performances.

Stuart Ostrow, a highly intelligent person who knew how to produce, arranged an interview for me with Mike Nichols, who was about to direct his first musical, *The Apple Tree*. Mr. Ostrow's project was a unique evening of three one-act musicals: *The Diaries of Adam and Eve* based on the Mark Twain story written by Sheldon Harnick and Jerry Bock, *The Lady or the Tiger* also by them, and *Passionella* written by Jules Feiffer. My interview with Mr. Nichols, at his three-story domed penthouse apartment in the Beresford on Central Park West, went well. I spent most of the meeting talking to him from another room, as he explained it took him quite some time to get dressed. I later learned he suffered from a rare childhood medical problem which left him totally hairless. He finally appeared, quite a handsome fellow, and we exchanged views on the material. He was very informative regarding the show (the project came about via Feiffer who started the whole thing and Nichols owed him a collaboration) and he had quite a grasp on all aspects of production. We laughed when he confided to me that he hated musicals. Even though this was his first, he allowed that with me and the writers looking over his shoulder, we would have some fun and get the job done. He agreed with my rehearsal schedule, and I landed a wonderful position with Mike Nichols.

We needed three people to carry the show, two men and a leading actress. Barbara Harris, who had worked with Mike in Chicago in their early days, was quickly set, and Larry Blyden, a popular Hollywood emigrant, followed. We auditioned everybody; I mean *everybody*. Notably, relatively unknown aspirants like Dustin Hoffman and Richard Gere read for us but got a friendly "*Next.*" Mike remembered Hoffman and later cast him in *The Graduate*. Finally, Alan Alda knocked us out and the show was set. Rehearsal with Mike Nichols is a class in direction. He brought with him an aura of rare intelligence, a warm rapport with the company, a firm grip on the material, and fun, fun, fun. Anecdotes fly all day mixed with stories and improvisations. Painlessly, the work got done, however, it appeared to me that most of the show was mediocre at best, and I was not catching Mike with a smash.

When we got to Boston for the first dress rehearsal, I took the curtain up on cue and immediately Mike called me out on stage.

"I hired you because you were touted as the best. The best stage manager does not take the curtain up on an empty stage," said Mike.

"Alan's in the tree, just as we rehearsed it," I replied.

"Where? I don't see him. Wave, Alan. Wave your arms," continued Mike.

And wave he did, from the glorious incandescent Garden of Eden that Tony Walton had designed, the same Tony Walton I met when Julie Andrews introduced him as her husband back in the *My Fair Lady* days. The sets were beautiful translucent animals lit from within and glowing in the dark. When arranged as figures in the Garden of Eden, they became a lightbox in which no human could be seen. Thankfully that wasn't my fault.

Mike stood staring at the stage, finagling, and turning to Stuart Ostrow seated in the empty theater.

Mike quietly said, "Stuart, I am about to make you a courageous producer."

Without waiting for an answer, Mike had me clear the stage, shoving thousands of dollars' worth of Tony's fabulous zoo into the alley.

"Let's play this first piece on an empty stage with just a ladder exactly as we did in rehearsals," continued Mike.

And so, we did. Later, Tony gave me a framed rendering of what the set might have been. The reviews were up and down, but regarding Barbara, the critics were unanimous in extolling her virtues, declaring her one of the most extraordinary talents to be seen in years. Little did they know the problem we had, and it was major trouble at that. Barbara Harris, a very beautiful and wonderful actress, had the world's worst case of stage fright in America. I'm not sure even Mike Nichols knew a cure, but he was a certifiable genius, world-class psychologist, and all-around theater guru, who would do some magical shenanigans in her dressing room and got her to somehow try. Most nights she would leave her room with tears still wet on her face, go onstage, and perform beautifully. Mike was not going to be around much, in fact, he had plans to leave soon after the New York opening to do *The Graduate*, leaving me with Barbara, and I didn't have a rabbit in my hat. She was a big hit in the show, a full house draw with the public. On the odd day, when she had control of that strange, uncontrollable malady, stage fright, she would deliver a performance of immense nuance and virtuosity. In 1967, she won the Tony Award as Best Actress in a Musical, *The Apple Tree*.

Mike did drop in often, once on a break from filming *The Graduate*, he reminded us that Dustin Hoffman auditioned for the Adam role and told us he was worth the price of admission in the movie. He also regaled us with an anecdote before he left: they were filming the montage showing Benjamin's boredom and in the section in the kitchen while he's making a sandwich the toaster accidentally popped startling Dustin. Mike got the idea that as the toaster popped and the toast flew out, a bird sitting on the window-sill would grab the toast and fly away. Everybody laughed, but the intention was that it would allude to Benjamin's desire to fly away. They brought the animal wrangler onto the set and explained the shot to him. The more they talked and the more they challenged the wrangler, time became a problem. They were all standing around expensively doing nothing. Finally, Mike asked the guy if the trick could be done.

"Sure," the wrangler said. Mike was ecstatic.

"You can train the bird to do this on cue?" Mike asked.

"Absolutely," the wrangler responded.

"Great. Time's a wasting. We're all standing around here. Everything is set. How soon can you get the bird over here?" Mike asked.

"Five weeks," the wrangler replied.

José Ferrer & Florence Henderson. Photo courtesy of Playbill

Mark
Hellinger
Theatre

PLAYBILL

the national magazine for theatregoers

DEAR
WORLD

Angela Lansbury. Photo courtesy of Playbill

4

**Harold Pinter. Miloš Forman.
Marlene Dietrich. Jules Feiffer.
Peter Ustinov. Angela Lansbury.
Peter Glenville.**

Alex Cohen decided I would be his permanent production stage manager. However, I could do other projects when the Cohen office was quiet with one exception: any Merrick show was off-limits. It was a great arrangement and Biff was, as it happens, doing the same thing with Merrick. Another part of my deal stipulated that I was to go to London and bring back theatrical productions Mr. Cohen had bought. It was a cushy job because I got to spend a great deal of time on the West End enjoying theater. The first production we brought over wasn't a play at all, but an *Evening with Flanders and Swann*, featuring two hilarious players doing pantomime and original songs, which was a big hit in London, but not in New York. We followed with *Black Comedy*, a funny play by Peter Shaffer, where light and dark are reversed. The evening started as an ordinary British comedy played in the dark when the stage lights ostensibly fail, and the actors play as if in the dark with the audience in light. It was a hit and ran for a year with Geraldine Page, Lynn Redgrave, and Michael Crawford, who would go on to fame wearing that silly mask in *The Phantom of the Opera*.

Like a true P.T. Barnum, Mr. Cohen magically made a deal with the American Theatre Wing and the Broadway League to televise the Tony Awards, LIVE from a Broadway Theater. We would air the show from a theater using the most minimal scenery so the installation of Tony scenery and technical equipment would cause the least trouble. I was production supervisor and associate producer of the very first telecast and did the show for seventeen years from 1967 until 1984 when I went to California. As far as the first telecast was concerned, a live broadcast from a Broadway Theater had never been done before. After the Saturday night performance ended, we would take any scenery of that show, store it on the loading dock or in the alley, and bring in the Tony scenery and the equipment for the telecast, including the stage lighting needed for enhancement. Once that was completed, sound and lighting needed to be refocused. We needed to be ready by 10 a.m. on Sunday morning for rehearsals. By 9 p.m., we would be on the air live. If I failed at that schedule, I would be taken out and shot. We decided to do the telecast from the Shubert Theatre mainly because I was the stage manager of *The Apple Tree*, which was playing there at the time, and the show had practically no scenery to get in the way.

As soon as the audience left after *The Apple Tree* performance, we began the event. The instant the theater doors opened to let the technical equipment into the theater, there was a work stoppage. The business agent of Local One of the Stagehands Union (IATSE) attempted to bar technicians from NABET (the TV union), to bring television equipment into the theater. A new accommodation had to be made, and damn fast. WABC, the network airing the show, sent their top lawyer, Steve Solomon. NABET joined the fracas and a solution was agreed upon. All cabling, electrical, and sundry items would be brought to the theater wall where stagehands would bring them into the theater. No NABET personnel would handle scenic or stage items, but they could assist in the set-up. The actual cameras and switchboards used for the telecast were totally NABET. Everybody shook hands and off we went. The combined crew was an absolute miracle. By 10 a.m. we were ready, and all scheduled cast and presenters went through their paces, and the actual live event was terrific. When it opened with Joel Grey, the MC from *Cabaret*, singing "Willkommen," we were all thrilled at the accomplishment.

We did the show mostly without any problems, except the 1977 show which was done during a NABET (TV technicians) strike. They formed a picket line in Shubert Alley. Everyone crossed the line and ABC sent Steve Solomon and his cohort, Richard Hockman, to keep order. Hockman turned out to be the funniest lawyer in captivity, and the time spent that night with him and Steve was a lifesaver. Shakespeare may have been right when he said: "The first thing we do is, let's kill all the lawyers." but he didn't know Richard and Steve, who have remained lifelong friends of mine. During the years doing the event, it was great directing traffic with the likes of Julie Andrews, Shirley MacLaine, Henry Fonda, Cicely Tyson, Ed Asner, Johnny Carson, Jane Fonda, Fred Astaire, Mikhail Barishnikov, Dustin Hoffman, and so many others.

We finished off that 1967 season with Harold Pinter's *The Homecoming*, which won Best Play and Best Actors, Ian Holm and Paul Rogers. The play was, and is, difficult to describe, but the feeling of a lurking menace among the dynamic family made for a fabulous evening. There were no rehearsals since we brought the entire production and cast over from London. They were a boisterous group, lots of fun, and many of them had never been to the States.

One night in a Boston bar, I asked Harold Pinter, "Harold, what is this play really about? It's driving me nuts."

"Father knows best," responded Harold, smiling as he proceeded to down his pint.

While the Cohen Office was recovering from all that activity, Arthur Cantor, a friend of Phil Adler, called. He was producing a two-character play and offered me a job. Being out of work, I went off to do *The Little Black Book* by Jean-Claude Carriere and directed by Miloš Forman; it was to be his first production in America. I went to the Chelsea Hotel where he and Jean-Claude were staying. The meeting was a riot. Mr. Forman had a thick Slavic accent and Mr. Carriere's accent was French. Between the two of them, I struggled to understand a thing. In the cast, they had Richard Benjamin and Delphine Seyrig, who had been fabulous in The *Day of the Jackal*. That was certainly a great start, and the production matters were settled quickly. Jean-Claude gave me a copy of the play as I left. I read it on the way home, and I was mortified. Two unnamed people meet in someone's apartment and sexually tantalize each other for two hours. That was it. Mr. Cantor, as I signed on, was enthusiastic regarding the language and situation in the play.

We rehearsed the play in the old Broadway Studios on West 47th Street. There were many sexual innuendos, confrontations, and tensions in the work. It was a weird and confounding rehearsal period, and Miloš and the cast didn't help. There was a gaggle of accents that left me perplexed. Days went by with the same unspoken confusion, and I finally slipped a note to Bob Borod, my assistant on the play. It read "LFOW." We could now enjoy ourselves while rehearsals were moving along with Bob trying all ways to decipher the cryptic "LFOW." I took him out of his misery just before we left for Philadelphia: LFOW (LOOK FOR OTHER WORK). Unfortunately cryptic, but true.

The put in went very well, the dress rehearsal was clean and neat. Even on the stage, in a gorgeous set by Oliver Smith, I had little sense of what the hell this crazy play was about. The whole group seemed confident, so I began to think there was something wrong with me. Our first preview was on a Wednesday, and the performance was going quite well. The audience was quiet which usually means they're listening. During intermission Miloš came back and said he had arranged with the house manager to ring the audience back in at exactly fifteen minutes since it was going so well. It seemed I was all alone in my dilemma. I checked on the house manager through the passageway door, and he was just ringing the audience back in. I called the cast on stage for the second act and in ten minutes, I checked the manager again. He was there at the back of the house seeming to stare into space. *Wake up!* At thirteen minutes he hadn't moved but was staring into the theater. I figured there must have been a problem in the auditorium, so I pushed aside one of the side curtains, and I was shocked: the theater was empty! Not a living soul had come back for the second act! The audience was gone! No, wait, there was a couple on the balcony having a little lunch. What was I to do? Miloš was nowhere to be found so the only thing I could do was play the second act to the couple in the balcony, enjoying their picnic.

We played the rest of the week with minor attendance, nobody mentioned the curious tale of the fleeing audience, and I could only shake my head at the "theatrical first" we had accomplished. A week later, we opened at the Helen Hayes Theatre in New York. Our best review by Clive Barnes said: ". . . foolish little play without either wit or humanity" and "The plot is cut so thin the author—if there was one—could probably make a decent living in the delicatessen business slicing sandwiches."[4] The show closed a week later, I had left for other work, and poor Bob Borod was cited as stage manager

4 Barnes, Clive. 1972. "Stage: 'The Little Black Book' Opens." *The New York Times*, April 26, 1972. https://www.nytimes.com/1972/04/26/archives/stage-the-little-black-book-opens-benjamin-miss-seyrig-at-the-helen.html.

in those lousy reviews. The notice named him as Robert Bored, a misprint but totally accurate.

It was time to get back to Alex Cohen. He had optioned a play by Jules Feiffer called *Little Murders*, a crazy satire on the meaningless violence of contemporary New York life. We cast a terrific group of actors: Barbara Cook, Elliot Gould, and David Steinberg who would become a popular television director and commentator. It was April 1967, and we did a couple of weeks of previews; the meaningless violence of critics closed us after seven performances. Shame, it was some of Mr. Feiffer's best work.

Enter Marlene Dietrich who Alex had seen in London and decided to bring to New York for a five-week run. For this limited run, Ms. Dietrich brought with her Burt Bacharach, pianist and conductor, who appeared with her onstage; Joe Davis, London's leading lighting designer; two stage managers (not including me); two dresses, a makeup supervisor, a hair supervisor, a security man, and an escort. There were so many people running around backstage, I thought I was in the way. We were booked into the Lunt-Fontanne Theater, and the day I met Ms. Dietrich in her dressing room she was on her knees cleaning the bathroom floor, scrubbing everything down. She obviously had a clean fetish, something to remember. She was amazingly cooperative and followed my every cue. With all her personnel buzzing around her, she appeared from her room, not the elderly Germanic cleaning lady I had met that day, but a glamorous, famous film star adorned in fabulous furs. The music anticipated her entrance, the lights dimmed, and the spotlight found her as she appeared dragging her white ermine behind her, so we called her "The Singing Hun." She played the five weeks to full houses and huge crowds waited for her at the stage door. Always on time and prompt to perform, it was a pleasure to be with her. Even Mr. Bacharach, a notable composer and performer in his own right, enjoyed her company and forgave a few musical glitches which were part of her charm. So, an event I initially had great trepidations about turned out fine. Me schmoozing with one of the great Hollywood legends turned out to be fascinating.

Rumors were floating around that Phil Adler was out-of-town with a musical disaster (I think it was *Baker Street*). I called to commiserate:

"How are you, Dad?" I asked.

"Well, we're in big trouble," he said.

"We've been there before. What's the plan?" I asked.

"Okay. Plan A—we finish the run here in Boston and close it up. Plan C—We finish here, open in New York, and probably get killed," he responded.

"You left out Plan B. What happens in Plan B?" I asked.

He responded, "It's got something to do with fire!" A little humor in the face of catastrophe. Just like my father.

Peter Ustinov's play, *The Unknown Soldier and His Wife*, which was announced to be the premier production to play the newly finished Vivian Beaumont Theater in Lincoln Center, New York. It was interesting, with an intriguing title and was a very theatrical play. Having Mr. Ustinov around made my days easier, however, that constant pain in my neck, John Dexter, was set to direct. The cast was fabulous, headed by Christopher Walken and Tommy Lee Jones, and including Brian Bedford, Howard Da Silva, Bob Dishy, and Don Scardino, who went on to be a popular director himself. The great experience was helping to establish the Beaumont as part of Lincoln Center. We ran for three months with very receptive reviews and then moved to the George Abbott Theatre (about to be razed for a commercial building) where we ran for two months more. I put up with Dexter and enjoyed the grief the cast put him through, and I loved being around Ustinov, a true friend. Funny, we opened one theater and closed another.

All of us have heard the expressions: "How in God's name did this boring thing get produced?" Or, "How is it possible that people have invested in this trash?" Or "Didn't they know this thing is awful?" I'll tell you a secret: *wishful thinking*. It was wishful thinking when Jerry Herman brought an idea to Alex Cohen that *The Madwoman of Chaillot*, a flimsy play by Maurice Valency, would make a great musical. Mr. Herman got Jerome Lawrence and Robert E. Lee to do the book to the musical now called *Dear World* (for some odd reason). They played parts of it for many backers and raised thousands of dollars (millions in today's dollars) and eventually hired Lucia Victor, a savvy young woman to direct her first Broadway production. The one truly terrific idea was to get Angela Lansbury to play Countess Aurelia, the Madwoman of Chaillot. We were so top tier a group, everyone had an assistant. Everyone! So many you couldn't turn around without falling over one. By count there were seven of them and even Lucia, who was our director had two (what they did was a mystery to me). In addition to Ms. Lansbury, we had two other Madwomen, Jane Connell and Carmen Mathews. Milo O'Shea played the Sewerman. There were thirty-five in the company, three standbys and ten understudies. When I got them all together it looked like a meeting of the House of Representatives. It was going to take the *raviest* raves to carry this load.

After the first week there were troubles brewing; Lucia had a concept in mind, and it didn't sit well with Angela. Result: they fired Lucia and got Peter Glenville to replace her. Peter and Angela got along well, so we got the show ready for Boston and when we arrived, Mr. Glenville quit. He claimed his contract enabled him to leave after six weeks and since he wasn't feeling well, he was out and on the next train. Happily, we got Joe Layton to direct and choreograph, leaving Donald Saddler, our original choreographer on the same train with Glenville. Joe, a veteran Broadway person, pulled everything together and with wishful thinking in our pocket, we opened in Boston for our first out of town tryout.

It was a bomb. No matter what they did during the pre-Broadway tryouts in Boston and Philadelphia, it just laid there. Angela was a stalwart lady, adjusting every night as new material was injected into this dying quail of Parisian nonsense. The problem was that *Chaillot* simply was not a musical idea and could never work no matter how much wishful thinking you threw at it. The production was lavish, the performances were wonderfully unique, but none of this entertained our audiences. They even brought in Cy Feuer for advice. Cy, a renowned producer, director, and winner of a lifetime Tony Award for excellence in theater, helped a bit but even he, caught up in this Parisian mishmash, wouldn't know a demitasse from a pastrami sandwich. The critics all liked Jerry Herman's score. Unfortunately, you can't go out singing the costumes. In 1969, Clive Barnes wrote a review for the *New York Times* in which he said ". . . no connoisseur of musical comedy can afford to miss Miss Lansbury's performance. It is lovely."[5] We played three months on Broadway, with Ms. Lansbury giving her level best, which is saying something. It's a lesson: wishful thinking will get you every time.

---

5 Barnes, Clive. 1969. "Theater: 'The Madwoman of Chaillot' Set to Music; 'Dear World' Arrives at Mark Hellinger Angela Lansbury and Godreau Excel." *The New York Times*, February 7, 1969. https://timesmachine.nytimes.com/timesmachine/1969/02/07/77437919.html.

PLAYBILL
MAGAZINE

PLYMOUTH
THEATRE

"GOOD EVENING"

Some hits I did. Photo courtesy of Playbill

Another hit. Photo courtesy of Playbill

5

Katharine Hepburn. Michael Bennett. André Previn. Sir John Gielgud. Sir Ralph Richardson. Joan Rivers. Jerry Orbach. Sammy Cahn. Ian Richardson. George Rose.

After we closed, I got a call from Helen Strauss, who turned out to be Katharine Hepburn's personal assistant and chief organizer. Ms. Hepburn wished to meet me to discuss a musical she was intending to do. The chance to meet her was terrific and a date was set for the following week. That gave me a little time to dig up the facts since I hadn't heard of any Broadway project featuring Katharine Hepburn being planned. As it turned out, Alan Jay Lerner had written the book and lyrics about Coco Chanel with a music score by André Previn. It was a musical being produced by Frederick Brisson, a veteran Broadway man who had produced *The Pajama Game* and *Damn Yankees* among others. The candle on top of the cake: Michael Bennett was signed as choreographer! The opportunity to stage manage this star vehicle was tantalizing and so this meeting with Ms. Hepburn took on some weighty importance. Just to meet her was a blast. I had just seen her in *The Lion* *in Winter* stealing the picture from Peter O'Toole and Anthony Hopkins. She lived in a beautiful townhouse in the Turtle Bay area of the East 40th Streets in New York: I was surprised, I thought she lived permanently in California. Ms. Strauss let me in through the street level under the front steps. The whole room was designed for comfort and led to a private garden in the back. Not bad for a place maybe used two months a year, if that much. She came bounding down the steps, looking terrific in lounging clothing and acting like we were old friends.

We hugged, kissed on the cheek, and she said, "I didn't know you were such a big guy. I like it."

I guess I blanched because she flopped on an easy chair with one leg hanging on the arm and said, "Better to be big when you run a big rig."

We chatted a bit while I wondered if she wanted me to open the conversation about Coco. Helen brought lemonade like we were a couple out of *The Philadelphia Story*, and we got down to it. Freddy Brisson, an old friend she and "Spence" had often met when he was married to "Roz" Russell, had enticed her to do this show about Coco Chanel even though she never sang in public. I asked if she sang at all even in her shower and she replied, "Let's wait and see." After a few sessions with Alan Lerner plus the additional lure of staying in town for a while, she agreed to the project. Part of her agreement was control of certain aspects of the production, one of which was stage manager. She had met Bud Widney, Lerner's assistant, who was titled production supervisor (which I had agreed to) but she wanted "the best guy in town" to be with her day to day. Michael Bennett had recommended me, we hit it off, and that was that. Before I left, she mentioned she had insisted on Michael Benthall, a noted British director. Even though she knew the musical was really a fashion show, which Bennett was great at mounting, she wanted Benthall who "had wonderful taste." I left after more cheek-kissing, mine a little rosy.

The meeting with Frederick Brisson went very well. I knew he was intent on hiring me since Ms. Hepburn wanted me. Alan Jay wanted Bud Widney on the payroll, so Mr. Brisson suggested he have the title, "Production Supervisor," which I agreed to when they offered me what must have been the top salary as production stage manager at that time. I'm lousy at negotiations, but I never turn down a good deal. Michael Bennett handled all the auditions, and we finally ended up with twenty female dancers each lovely enough to be a runway model. The group included Ann Reinking in her first Broadway role and Graciela Daniel, now a Tony Award-winning director/choreographer. Six Principals as well as George Rose and Michael Allinson, who had both played Henry Higgins in the original *My Fair Lady,* were cast. In addition, we counted a dozen male singer/dancers in the production. A huge cast. Michael Benthall had not yet arrived from London for reasons I never knew.

Kate (she told me to call her that) was true to her word—she wasn't a singer, but André Previn worked with her on voice, established a vocal range that sounded quite usable, and Alan Lerner kept her songs within that range. The physical production was technically very complicated. The main set was Coco Chanel's apartment, Rue Cambon in Paris, constructed on a huge turntable, with a section of the table removed so that dancers showing the "Coco line" could emerge from below stage. It was frighteningly intricate because Michael staged those entrances as the table revolved the apartment into the showroom. There was danger each time if I blew a cue and turned the table too soon or too late. It turned out, by the way, that when Mr. Benthall finally arrived, his drinking habit made him useless most of the time. He kept a loyal rapport with Kate, and she was gentle and kind to him. They decided to open the show "cold" with no out-of-town performances but a longer series of previews at the Hellinger Theatre in town. We spent a week on dress rehearsals and technical run throughs. We were ready. Our first preview came on that following Monday and went on beautifully. The staff out front was delighted and Kate, by the second show, was beaming. Her favorite moment came in the second act right after the intermission which we carefully coordinated with House management so that the audience was seated before the curtain rose on Kate, alone in her apartment, singing a lullaby to her departed father who was the love of her life. It had not been anticipated that a skyscraper was in the process of being built directly across the street. The noise of construction was apparent, but the show almost drowned it all out. Once in a while, you could feel the theater shudder from the banging and, in general, the cacophony was disturbing, making everyone irritable. I feared Kate would go nuts if her lullaby was noisily interrupted, and sure enough the jackhammers were doing their dance right in the middle of her song. She finished the performance and sent Helen to bring me to her dressing room.

"What in heaven's name is going on," she fumed at me. "Is that building going up or coming down?"

I commiserated as much as I could, but what recourse did we have?

"I'll tell you what we can do, we can cancel the Wednesday matinee. That's what we can do. This is impossible."

She was serious, I could tell from her demeanor. I told her we couldn't possibly do that; we were already sold out. She told me to call the guys and tell them I want something done about the noise or cancel the matinees. I agreed to make the call and could see her cooling down. After a bit we were even chatting about how ridiculous it was, and chuckling. She suddenly jumped up from the couch and said:

"I know, Jerry. You go over there and tell them when I do the little song, they should stop work on the building." We laughed, and she said, "No, really. I bet they would do it."

I explained that canceling work for twenty minutes or so by that huge crew would probably be more expensive than canceling a matinee. She insisted and left me no other choice. It was nearly the end of their workday, so I practiced a bit of my fool's errand and went into the temporary office shed at the side of the worksite. The burly guy at the desk, surrounded by work plans and piles of paper, looked up questioningly.

I decided to plug right in, "I'm the stage manager of the show across the street and we have a problem with the noise coming from your construction bothering the audience and especially the performers." Before he could respond, I went on, "we realize there's not much you can do but we wondered if you could accommodate our star, Katharine Hepburn. She has a tiny song in the show and if, during her number, you could, if I alerted you, stop work on the building?"

That's about what I remember of my request of the superintendent, but I hesitate to write his reply. Suffice it to say if the word "fuck" was removed from our language, he would have been left speechless. I returned to Kate and explained how useless it all was. She asked me to call the office in the morning and have them do something. I agreed to do so, and we called it a long, frustrating night. Before I could reach the office the next morning, I got a call from Ralph Roseman, our company manager, who told me all had been arranged. I pressed him for more of the amazing details.

He said, "Amazing is a good word for it. Ms. Hepburn was at the building bright and early this morning. With the foreman in tow, she went up the exterior outdoor elevator and arranged a general meeting on the twelfth floor with the entire crew. So, here's the news, when you blow a whistle out the stage door, the building will take a coffee break catered by you-know-who."

So, for the entire run of the show, the Uris building had coffee and donuts for every matinee performance. She remained firm, mostly correct, never vindictive or overbearing, a total pro. I remember my favorite review by John S. Wilson, which summed her up completely: "She is Peter Pan . . . a virtuoso magician working with nothing but thin air and her own inner resources."[6] When we closed after a year's run, she gave me a self-portrait framed with the following words written on it: "Don't Forget Kate." How could I?

I wound up in London after *Coco* closed. I was assisting on the taping of Ms. Dietrich's television show and met up with Alex Cohen and his wife there. Afterward, we went to see a performance of *Home*, a play by David Storey, directed by the renowned Lindsay Anderson at the Royal Court Theatre. The play takes place in a mental institution, but that fact isn't revealed until later in the evening. The cast of four included Sir John Gielgud, Sir Ralph Richardson, Dandy Nichols, and Mona Washburne. The curtain rises on a rather rundown patio set with two outdoor chairs at a small table. Sir John casually enters and, after testing the weather, sits. A bit later Sir Ralph saunters in and after sighting Gielgud, he sits next to him. It appears they are relative strangers but are convivial. There ensues almost a half hour of a master class in acting. We sat there transfixed watching these two extraordinary actors chatting and mesmerizing us. There was no question, Alex was hooked and was going to bring the production to New York. It had to be seen.

Home opened to rave reviews in New York and settled in for a limited run. Sir John was the quintessential English gentleman,

---

6 Wilson, John S. 1970. "Hepburn's Hep but 'Coco' Isn't." *The New York Times*, February 15, 1970. https://nytimes.com/1970/02/15/archives/hepburns-hep-but-coco-isnt.html.

relaxing in his dressing room. Sir Ralph was heartier, riding to the theater on a motorcycle he had rented for the run of the play. The two ladies thought they were in Disneyland. One day, Dandy had a visitor from London seeing the matinee, so she asked me if I could reserve a quiet table at Sardi's restaurant across the street, and kindly invited me along. Dandy's friend, Athene Saylor, was an actress most everyone had worked with. Sir Ralph begged off, but the rest of us sat down at a table Mr. Sardi had reserved for us, a round table on the second floor of the restaurant. I was enjoying myself immensely, listening to conversation about how different it was for these English actors to work on Broadway as opposed to Shaftesbury Avenue. Somehow the chat zeroed in on actors and actresses you hate to work with. Everyone had a laughingly hilarious anecdote. I had a few myself but before I could join in, Gielgud broke in, a bit in his cups, and said:

"No one could endure what I have been through with Athene Saylor."

Thinking he was making a joke, we all kind of giggled.

"Not only once, but twice I've had to appear with this creature. You all know her. She's the one who absolutely destroyed my *Earnest*. How they allow her on stage is beyond me," he continued.

Good God, he's not kidding! How the hell can we stop him because he has no idea who's sitting right there in front of him. All eyes are on poor Athene, ashen with little tears on her cheeks. But he continued haranguing her:

"Talentless. Uncouth . . ."

His eyes had been circling the group and they finally landed on her.

"Never in my life, have I . . ."

It began to dawn on him. He appeared to be thinking, *is it really her? How do I get out of this? What can I possibly say?*

Looking straight into her eyes, absorbing her grief-stricken face, he said, "Oh, no! Not YOU, Athene!"

Man, I couldn't wait to get back to the theater. When I told Sir Ralph about the disaster at Sardi's, he laughed and almost rolled off his couch.

Just before *Home* closed, I wrote a note to Harold Pinter requesting the rights to direct the first off-Broadway production of his play *The Homecoming*. Remarkably he agreed and a young producer, Joel Schenker, signed on. I got a couple of expatriate Brits, Eric Berry and Tony Tanner, the wonderful Janice Rule, and a popular New York soap opera actor named Lawrence Keith. We spent three intense weeks examining the play and opened to positive reviews: The *Times* called it "a remarkable work in an admirable production."[7] It ran for some months; I was very proud of it.

It was always my good fortune to have Alex Cohen pop up just as I was looking for some interesting activity. He had a script called *Fun City* which was a satire on living in New York City, filled with jokes, puns, eccentricities, and general mayhem. It was written by a young up and coming comedienne, Joan Rivers, who was to appear in it. Coming after my good notices on the Pinter play, Alex asked me to direct it. In terms of plot and structure it wasn't really a play, but it was hilarious and with a little *wishful thinking* I thought we could get by the critics and entertain our audience. I cast a group of wonderfully eccentric actors to surround Joan, who turned out to be a total surprise as an actress and everything looked promising. We opened the day after New Year's, the audience laughing all night, but the critics weren't buying it. They knew it wasn't Broadway material and they panned it mercilessly. It was so bad

---

7 Gussow, Mel. 1971. "Theater: 'The Homecoming' Revived." *The New York Times*, May 19, 1971. https://nytimes.com/1971/05/19/archives/theater-the-homecoming-revived-janice-rule -and-tony-tanner-in-bijou.html.

they tore down the Morosco Theatre right after we did seventeen performances. Strike one for me as director.

The other script Alex had, and one I would have given my eye teeth to direct, was a play by Bob Randell, *6 Rms Riv Vu*, another city dramedy but this one was a play about real people struggling in a real situation. Two couples looking to find a rental apartment on the Upper West Side of Manhattan, unexpectedly meet in the barren living room of one. We soon learn from their embarrassed behavior that they had been married to each other, the wife of one of the couples to the husband of the other. Much is revealed, many secrets aired, and despite some hilarious interruptions, peace slowly descends. Sad for me but happily for the production, the project came with a director involved. Ed Sherin and his very talented wife, Jane Alexander, had brought the play to the Cohen office. We eventually cast Jerry Orbach as the man once married to Jane and Ron Harper and Jennifer Warren to complete the mix-up. It was also F. Murray Abraham's introduction to Broadway, substituting both men. All went swimmingly and we opened to very positive notices. The *Times* critic John J. O'Connor said: "The old formula is generously spiked with several fresh touches."[8] The play ran for almost nine months and created one of show business' most rollicking poker games. Orbach, an inveterate gambler, played host in his dressing room and had a dedicated group of players from other shows. I'm not a gambler, except as my profession demands, but I loved to kibbutz. The show moved from the small Helen Hayes Theatre where we had three months to the much larger Lunt-Fontanne mainly due to ticket demand, but Mr. Orbach insisted we did it to make room for the game.

---

8 O'Connor, By John J. 1974. "TV: A Nicely. Done '6 Rrns Riv Vu.'" *The New York Times,* March 16, 1974. https://www.nytimes.com/1974/03/16/archives/tv-a-nicely-done-6-rms-riv-vu.html.

Hildy Parks Cohen had fond memories of a British revue called *Beyond the Fringe* and persuaded Alex Cohen to contact Alan Bennet, the main force behind the original, to do an updated version tentatively entitled *Behind the Fridge*. Bennett had become a noted author and film director and had no interest in the idea. However, Peter Cook, coming off a tour of a comedy act called "Dud and Pete," contacted the office offering the services of Dudley Moore and Peter Cook from the original *Fringe* revue. Thus, was born *Good Evening,* a comedy in twelve acts.

I left *6 Rms* towards the end of its run and went to London with the idea of working with Cook and Moore on fashioning enough material to fill a Broadway show. Alex had offices atop the Queen's Theatre, and I arranged to meet the guys up there as often as possible. The meetings were ad lib and I recorded every word they spoke, which were many both of them being nonstop talkers. They performed their "Dud and Pete" cabaret act for me and I found two pieces we could use, one from the original *Fringe* production, but mainly we tried to find new satirical sketches and musical ideas that would create a show. They were an ideal comic pair, Peter standing at six foot two, and Dudley at five foot three.

It was great to spend time in London on a per diem, living in a flat on Smith Street near Parliament and touristing around on days off. I saw the gamut of plays on Shaftesbury, had backstage visits at the National Theatre, and watched the final touches made of The Globe, a recreation of Shakespeare's Theatre. What a life! Meanwhile the work at the Queen's was going very well. We met at least twice a week, while I spent much of the down time typing out the tape recordings made during the improvisations. Dudley made the final corrections bringing in Peter to flesh out the scripts. At the end of almost a month, we had six comedy gems and two Dud and Pete dialogues we could use. Dudley was creating two musical pieces and

Peter promised to add a monologue of his own. Just a day before I left for home, Peter came through with a wonderful addition and, as they were celebrating leaving the Queen's office, they suddenly added the climatic masterpiece, "The Frog and Peach."

In New York I spent some time with Bob Randolph on the running order and scenic design. Alex remembered some famous items from *Fringe,* and we made Joe McGrath, a filmmaker, design two sequences for the show based on *Fringe.* The duo arrived soon after and in a breathless surge, we put the whole thing together. Alex insisted we call it *Good Evening,* and the show opened to rave reviews. Clive Barnes wrote, "I started laughing at the beginning, and I ended laughing at the end, and unless you are even more miserable than a critic, you will, too. These two men are mad, funny and truthful."[9] It ran for over a year and won special Tony Awards. Sadly, these two comic geniuses came to very tragic ends. Whatever demons Cook endured, his drinking habit contributed to his early death at fifty-eight years old. Dudley's illness, untreatable progressive supranuclear palsy, left him unable to care for himself. His death came in 2002, his fabulous brain having evaporated. We had some great times together. May they rest in peace.

In the same genre as *Good Evening,* we all had the idea of bringing Sammy Cahn's evening at the New York YMCA to Broadway. Mr. Cahn, an Academy Award-winning lyricist, songwriter, and winner of a lifetime Emmy in music, was very interested so we filled out the program, added three singers to appear with him, and set the whole production to look like we were in Sammy Cahn's living room. He had an easy charm and delighted audiences in what the show really was about: "and then I wrote . . ." It was named *Words and Music.*

---

9 Barnes, Clive. 1973. "Theater: 'Good Evening.'" *The New York Times,* November 15, 1973. https://www.nytimes.com/1973/11/15/archives/theater-good-evening-zany-peter-cook-and-dudley-moore-return-the.html.

Certainly a lightweight production but so enjoyable it ran for five months and made an enormous profit.

At about the same time, the industrious Mr. Cohen met Peter Ustinov in France while on vacation. Mr. Ustinov, a two-time Oscar winner, famous writer, journalist, and raconteur had just finished writing a play and discussed it with Alex, who was totally impressed with Mr. Ustinov (who wouldn't be?). They agreed to bring it to New York, backed financially by Bernard Delfont, a leading London producer, and starring Peter Ustinov himself. The political satire was set in the waiting room of Hell, with characters reminiscent of Nixon, Khrushchev, and a young assassin who had killed them both. We cast Mr. Ustinov as the Russian, Joseph Sommer as the American, and Beau Bridges, in his first and only appearance on Broadway, as the gun-toting killer. Olympia Dukakis and Joseph Maher joined the cast, completing the stellar group. Ellis Rabb, who had just won a Tony for directing, was brought on to direct the play. Unfortunately, the project was done in haste and the satire was thin, but the jokes were wonderful. Rehearsals were as funny as the play. Ustinov was brilliant at his best. Directing him (poor Ellis Rabb) was like halting a runaway train. We never gave Peter time to examine the play's potential, to do needed rewrites, and to really finish the work. As a result, the critics recognized its potential, missed it, and we closed.

What's better than having a totally fabulous smash hit on Broadway? Doing it again, sometimes. I had been directing revivals of My Fair Lady during the Summer Stock seasons. Good ones with Edward Mulhare, Anne Rogers, and Ray Milland, an Oscar winner in his first musical. I was preparing to do one for the Denver Light Opera company and was asked to use as many locals as possible. As a result, there were fifty couples at the Covent Garden opening scene and a like number at Ascot. There were a few productions but it's better we forget them.

Herman Levin, the producer and owner of the first-class rights, wanted to do a twentieth-year anniversary revival of *My Fair Lady* on Broadway, being an exact replica of the original. I was the only one of the staff that was connected to that production, so I was set to direct the revival. I suggested Crandall Diehl, who was our dance captain, to do the choreography. Scenery was to be built according to Oliver Smith's blueprints and the chorus would wear the costumes that had been in storage, but the principals' costumes would be constructed anew. We had the great good luck to sign Ian Richardson to play Higgins, Robert Coote was still available for Pickering, and George Rose, a popular favorite character actor, to do Doolittle. Our one tough decision was casting Eliza Doolittle. The only one who came close to handling Eliza's three necessaries of a Cockney accent, a warm British accent, and a voice capable of delivering the character's extraordinary range was Christine Andreas, who we knew from *Words and Music*. Casting was completed when we hired Brenda Forbes, a fine Broadway veteran, to play Higgins's mother, and Jerry Lanning, a tall, handsome actor with a wonderful tenor voice to be the lovelorn Freddy Eynsford-Hill. Getting the production up on its feet was blindingly simple since both Crandall and I had done it so often. This offered us time to concentrate on the performance. Ian Richardson was extraordinary as Higgins, bringing an intelligence and vitality to the role. He was also a great help to Christine when we worked on their scenes together, as he voiced a terrific Cockney accent for Christine to copy. George Rose, who had never done a musical, rehearsed like a kid who had found a new toy. All in all, it was a happy and productive period, full of cooperation and brimming with talent.

In terms of our mission, the play was an exact copy of Moss Hart's direction. I did make one exception, a vital moment at the opening of Act Two, one that I had wanted to do in light of the feminist movement and that held dramatic importance for the finale of the piece. It occurs as the group returns from the ball where Eliza had made a triumph. Pickering and the servants are exulting and congratulating Higgins for his great success while everyone ignores Eliza standing mute at the side. Finally, all exit for the night leaving Higgins and Eliza alone. Still celebrating himself, he brusquely asks Eliza to fetch him his slippers, which she promptly throws at him, demanding recognition. Totally dismissive of her feelings, he heads for bed. Eliza reminds him she is wearing rented jewelry which must be returned lest she "be charged with stealing." Sensing the sarcasm in her voice, he demands that she "*hand them over!*" It was at this point in Moss's staging that Eliza crosses the room and gives the jewels to Higgins.

I had always felt the opposite and staged it differently a number of times. I had Eliza hold her ground, offer the bunch of jewels defiantly, and wait. After a dramatic moment, Higgins is forced to cross to her, snatch the outstretched pack of jewels, and find some face-saving way to exit the room. It immediately dramatized her new independence and stature. It also gives the Higgins actor much to play with. All of this resolved itself into a kind of shift in character development which ends with "I've Grown Accustomed to Her Face." In the final scene when Eliza returns to a lonely Higgins, he doesn't rush to her, but we sense he would love to; Alan Lerner wrote the perfect ending. If Higgins hadn't changed, he would have said:

"Eliza, bring me my slippers."

Instead, recognizing the new relationship, he says: "Eliza, where the devil are my slippers?" The perfect ending.

The reviews were excellent, despite a little unnecessary carping over Christine's performance as if wanting Julie Andrews instead but recognizing the overall quality of the revival. In the end, George

Rose won the Tony Award for best performance by a leading actor in a musical, and Ian Richardson was nominated in the same category. The show ran for a year and made a profit. Mission accomplished.

An old friend of mine, Ken Myers, had the rights to a comedy about death, and asked if I would read it. The idea certainly was intriguing, and the script titled *Checking Out* was a little thin but very funny. A hale and hearty man in his mid-eighties decides he will end his life before illness, pain, or dementia can cripple him, so he plans a farewell party to which he invites his family and old friends. There ensues many humorous events and discussions as everyone tries to talk him out of it. He counters with some sage-like opinions and holds to the notion, "why not plan your memorial before you're too far gone to enjoy it?" The characters were all too familiar, but the situations were quite hilarious and, in total, it made for an entertaining evening with a bit of soul searching to boot. It was originally planned as a two-week engagement at the Greenwich Playhouse in Connecticut. If it played well there, it could quite inexpensively be brought into town. There goes wishful thinking again! We ended with a very fine cast, comprising a wacky Jewish family and a couple of friends: Allen Swift, the author, took on the leading character, his daughter was played by Joan Copeland (Arthur Miller's sister), and his sons were played by Mason Adams and Hy Anzell. The psychiatrist who tries to talk him out of his planned suicide, once the party is over, was Larry Bryggman, a very popular Broadway performer. The rest of the group was composed of Michael Gorrin, Jonathan Moore, and Tazewell Thompson.

Maybe it was the lovely summer nights, maybe it was my fabulous direction, or perhaps the sharply funny performance, but the play was a huge success in Connecticut which prompted management to take the whole thing to Broadway. Allen agreed, and much to my regret, I did too. The reviews in New York labeled us something like, "a hysterical sitcom but not a Broadway venture," and we closed in two weeks when our ardent producers ran out of funds. Strike two on my director's resume.

Adler directing Olivier at the Tony Awards.

Having fun making the cast album of Coco *with Katharine Hepburn*

6 | Richard Rodgers. Liv Ullmann.
Richard Harris. Richard Burton.
Christine Ebersole. Debbie Allen.
Leslie Uggams. Richard Conte.
Richard M. Nixon.

Meanwhile, Alex Cohen was getting involved in a new work by Richard Rodgers, who was fighting a battle with cancer. He had constructed a musical with Martin Charnin, who had a big hit with *Annie* and had cowritten the book with Thomas Meehan. They had based the work on the play *I Remember Mama* by John Van Druten. The veteran Cy Feuer was going to direct, and the international Norwegian film star, Liv Ullmann, was to play Mama. The supporting cast was headed by the renowned George Hearn as Papa and included George S. Irving as Uncle Chris and Ian Ziering as her son, Nils. The huge cast of dancers and singers were to be staged by Danny Daniels. I had a terrific assistant, Robert Bennett, and a third assistant, Christopher Cohen, a young and eager fledgling.

As always, the start of rehearsals was exciting and hopeful. We coordinated the schedule beautifully and ran the musical staging and book rehearsals in close harmony. Our only problem, so far as I could see, was Ms. Ullmann showed no aptitude in singing, which is certainly a stumbling block for a person starring in a musical! Special time was allotted for Jay Blackton, our music director, to work with Liv during rehearsals that were usually attended by Mr. Rodgers. I was not privy to their success with her, but those sessions took away from important book rehearsals. Slowly, we put it all together and though slightly unprepared, we went off to Philadelphia for previews. Another problem, as we discovered in Philadelphia, was in a large auditorium you had trouble understanding Liv Ullmann's accent. We were in great shape: we had a star who couldn't sing, dance, let alone be understood! To solve these hindrances, Jay Blackton and his associate, Uel Wade, took her in hand and forged a workable performance, and as she became more confident the character became quite usable. She was never a warm, lovable Mama, but an icy, unlovable stage matriarch. We all had visions of Mady Christians (with Marlon Brando in his debut) onstage and Irene Dunne in the film version, but we all dug in and encouraged her. As she gained confidence, she also gained hoggish. For example, she attempted to take a new song that was being written for Mr. Hearn as her own. Finally, Marty Charnin berated her in her dressing room:

"Liv, what is this? You can't sing every song in the show!"

She responded, seriously, "Why not?"

She also took to demanding certain choristers be fired. It was some strange phobia she had, accusing individuals of smirking behind her back, causing disruptions backstage, and generally making a nuisance of themselves. Management gave into her odd behavior, and we replaced four people for absolutely no reason. The work in Philadelphia was in fits and starts; cuts and changes were rehearsed during the day while performances continued at night. Some of the changes affected scenes that were ultimately kept in the musical. For example, dances were altered in some cases because the music they reflected was changed. It was all part of the usual hodgepodge of being pre-Broadway. Liv and the company handled the old and new material well, but I can't say the same for our audiences who struggled to keep up with some really confusing moments. However, the critics recognized a work in progress and gave us encouraging notices.

The New York critics were not so generous but respected our creators, setting us up for an average run of a hundred performances—more than I think we deserved. The reviews were kind to Mr. Rodgers and Martin Charnin, but devastating to Ms. Ullmann, calling her "unsuited to the stage," and "hopelessly lost."[10] In the face of that diatribe, she did her best night after night. She kept the company and staff at arm's length and remained aloof. I don't think we exchanged conversation after the opening, as she gave all her attention to Bob Bennett. The rest of the cast received very positive notices. In retrospect, I enjoyed my time with Cy Feuer and was honored to have been associated with Richard Rodgers, in what was his final production in a great career on Broadway.

I had just finished putting I Remember Mama to bed when Manny Azenberg called. Next to Phil Adler, Manny was the best general manager in the business and was moving on as a producer, which he was doing with Dasha Epstein and the Shubert Office. He had put together a fine group: Tom Conti to direct a play by Frank D. Gilroy starring Ed Flanders, Susan Kellermann, and J.T. Walsh. The play, Last Licks, was a sequel to The Subject Was Roses, which won Tony Awards and Oscars. Mr. Gilroy had struck up a friendship with Tom Conti, an actor and director known more in the UK than

---

10   Eder, Richard. 1979. "Stage: 'I Remember Mama.'" The New York Times, June 1, 1979. https://www.nytimes.com/1979/06/01/archives/stage-i-remember-mama-with-liv-ullmann.html.

here, but we found him utterly warm-hearted and in firm grasp of the material. He handled Mr. Flanders very gently, Ed being a recovering alcoholic. It had the most professional rehearsal periods I had ever experienced: an interesting play, good direction, a sensational cast, and the best assistant I ever had, Jonathan Weiss. The plot was simple; a son, realizing his father is mostly homebound since the mother has died some months previously, brings a caretaker to live in. The twist is that she and the father have had an ongoing affair for a few years. That's the play; funny in the first act but boring in the second act. The critics pounced on the second act, one calling it "turgid."[11] We did a week of previews followed by two weeks of performances, and we closed. It was a shame but without a star to attract an audience, it is impossible to recover from mixed reviews.

Somehow two neophytes, who happened to be eager and intelligent producers, Mike Merrick and Don Gregory, had acquired the road rights to *Camelot* and signed Richard Burton to reprise his role as King Arthur. With that name on the masthead, they quickly set up a six-month tour (with options to continue) with stops in six cities, playing a month in each city. Mr. Burton recommended Frank Dunlop, a well-respected director from London and got Buddy Schwab from the original to choreograph. Alan Lerner wanted me to go with the show and, even though I hadn't been on the road in almost forty years, I was presently at liberty. So, when they threw a pile of money at me, I accepted, and took Jonathan Weiss with me. The cast put together was in the main, first rate, and included Paxton Whitehead, James Valentine, Richard Muenz as Lancelot, and a cast of thirty-four singer/dancers. The only error that was made (and I never knew who made it) was for the role of Guinevere.

---

11   Kerr, Walter. 1979. "Play: Gilroy Drama Of Me, 'Last Licks.'" *The New York Times*, November 21, 1979. https://www.nytimes.com/1979/11/21/archives/play-gilroy-drama-of-age-last-licks.html.

I was among those who recognized from the start that our leading lady was miscast and felt that we should think about the situation carefully, admit the wrong, and recast. Management was adamant, and Richard was willing to give her a chance, so we worked through the first act.

The moment came, as I knew it had to; I think it was early in the second week, and everyone, including Frank Dunlop and Richard, was getting a little uncomfortable. The rehearsal was for the "What Do the Simple Folk Do?," a number involving Arthur, Guinevere, and some choristers. At the finish of the first chorus, she (I am opting to keep her nameless, since it wasn't her fault that she was miscast) unbelievably turned to Richard Burton and gave him a note! In front of everybody, she was correcting Richard Burton's performance! You have to have quite a resume to do that or a ton of chutzpah. There was a silence broken up by Frank who called: "Moving on."

By the end of that day, plans were made, auditions planned, and days were numbered for the replacement of our Guinevere, the costar of this production. Machinations had to be kept secret from the company, lest word were to get out and nasty rumors would invite much talk of trouble. Auditions began by the middle of that week; management and their casting person would coordinate with me, and sessions were planned at the end of rehearsals. We were at the Winter Garden Theatre and when the cast was gone, Jonathan, who had stashed the prospective costars in a little bar on the corner, would shuffle them in one at a time. The most we ever had was three in one day.

Rehearsals continued with (I'll call her Cathy, OK?) Cathy in place, the fear growing more intense the closer we came to the date of our leaving for Toronto. If we don't find a replacement soon, we would have to open with Cathy and suffer the consequences.

Miraculously, two days before we left town, in walked Christine Ebersole who simply wowed us. Frank Dunlop had a nice chat with her and was obviously impressed. We gave her a copy of the play, told her to look it over and return tomorrow to meet and possibly read with Mr. Burton. The next day we all gathered, and Christine absolutely hit a homer, reading a scene with Richard and singing. With his approval, Mike Merrick and Don Gregory took Christine away to finalize her contract. May I remind you, we had done our last rehearsal that afternoon and we had given the company travel instructions and they went off never the wiser. We later learned that we had a new Guinevere, and that the producers had gone to break the news to Cathy who, at that moment, was hosting a congratulations and farewell to Toronto party in her Greenwich Village apartment. Nobody deserves a slap like that, but at least the guys were sympathetic enough to go to her to soften the blow.

The next morning, the company met at the theater and boarded the airport bus to JFK. On the bus I made the announcement: "Ladies and Gentlemen, meet your new Guinevere, Christine Ebersole." There was a burst of cheers and applause, and off we went. I spent the whole trip to Toronto with her, checking her script and organizing her work schedule. Jonathan would teach her the blocking, run lines with her and generally give her any assistance she needed. All that activity took place in the basement of the theater as I put the show up and the company rehearsed with the orchestra in the lobby. Both Jonathan and I prayed she was a fast learner and a fearless performer. We need not to have worried, she was a sensation!

There was great chemistry between Richard and Christine and the cast, loaded with professionals. We were booked into six cities, a month's run in each. The cities were New York, Chicago, Dallas, New Orleans, San Francisco, and, finally, Los Angeles. Toronto as the break-in and all went exceedingly well. In June 1980, we opened at the State Theatre in Lincoln Center. Frank Rich in the *New York Times* wrote: "Who says that you can't go home again? Last night Richard Burton returned to the Kingdom of 'Camelot,' and it was as if he had never abdicated his throne. True, Mr. Burton is older now, but he remains every inch the King."[12] That was really true, thanks in the main to the care he was receiving from his new bride, Suzy Hunt Burton. Richard, a recovering alcoholic, needed all the help he would get from her, and he remained in fairly good health in spite of the rigor of eight physically challenging performances a week.

All that came crashing down one afternoon in New York. Somehow, Richard had lunch with his old drunk mate, Richard Harris. Theirs was a liquid lunch and by the time Richard was dropped off at the theater, he really dropped off. You had to take an elevator to get to the dressing room floor, which led to the stage. Richard was a little late for the matinee, unusual for him because Suzy was so prompt. When she told me he was having lunch with Richard Harris, a notorious walking tankard, I became anxious. At ten minutes past the half-hour, the elevator door opened, and Richard Burton staggered out. He fell across the hall, hitting himself on the bulletin board and starting to sing some Scottish folk song. I think it was Scottish, but in the situation I was in, who the hell cared? We were all in deep doo-doo. Cursing Richard Harris for getting him drunk before the show, Jonathan and I dragged the poor guy into his dressing room and plopped him down. Suzy was aghast and started undressing him as if he was sober. I was alerting his understudy, Bill Parry, to get ready to go on. The company was notified over our intercom. Suzy, hearing all this commotion, grabbed me and assured me that Richard would be ready to do the matinee.

---

12 Rich, Frank. 1980. "Stage: Burton Stars in Revival of 'Camelot'; In King Arthur's Court." The New York Times, July 9, 1980. https://www.nytimes.com/1980/07/09/archives/stage-burton-stars-in-revival-of-camelot-in-king-arthurs-court.html.

Sitting there, half in costume, still humming that damn song, the man was completely out of it.

Suzy said, "A little tea and cold compresses will do it. I guarantee it. We've done it before."

I said, "Suzy, a little tea? If he lit a cigarette, it would blow his head off. Come on, he's not here, he's off somewhere. He thinks he's in kilts, for heaven's sake! I can't take the chance."

She pleaded with me, tears running down her face, telling me that Richard had a terrible phobia, that missing a performance was nearing the end. I shook him up a bit, and he mumbled his readiness. I told Suzy we had twenty-five minutes to go and to pump that tea as fast as she could. What possessed me? Why did I go against every bone in my body? All my instincts told me he could never get through the show, but he was so pitiful, and she was so adamant and positive.

We started the show, the overture began, and Jonathan escorted Richard, who was perspiring, to his place onstage behind an entrance position. James Valentine, who was playing Merlin, was behind his rock, sweating worse than Burton, terrified about doing his scene with a puddle. On cue in the music, Jonathan nudged Richard who came out and strode to center stage, where he decided to entertain us by singing his favorite Scottish Hymn. What could I do? It was a full house and management frowns on refunds. It was a sad sight, and I had the house curtain pulled down. We took him back to his dressing room, still singing, but suddenly he was furious at me for pulling the curtain down. Later, Jonathan said he fell asleep as soon as he hit his chair. An announcement was made but it was obvious what had happened. Bill Parry gave a fine performance and amazingly Richard appeared as King Arthur that night, performing as if nothing had occurred. The news of his missing the matinee made the front page of the *New York Times* the next day. The great thing about touring with a star in a favorite show for a sold-out run is the total disregard the company has for critics and reviews. We were a hit wherever we went and that reflected in the performances we gave. When you play a monthly schedule in each city, one has time for rest, sightseeing and, of course, shopping. Most of all, there's time for rest, which Mr. B needed. You don't realize the effects of doing a play eight times a week, it's like running a marathon. I could see how it was slowly wearing Richard down. His behavior since the disaster in New York was exemplary; Suzy said he slept late and did the show, that's all. It seemed the cast buoyed his spirits, but the grind was taking its toll.

By the time we were finishing the San Francisco engagement, Mr. B was exhausted. It was a good show, with a much longer period for sleep and rest than before. Los Angeles was our last gig and no sooner than we opened there, I got a call from New York. It seems Burton had called our producer, Mike Merrick (actually, Suzy made the call), and requested an early end to his contract. He had discussed his exhaustion with Richard Harris, and the physical drain the show had caused him. Richard Harris agreed to step in if Burton left the show. Naturally Mr. Merrick was shocked and after a report from me on Burton's health, he asked if I was comfortable putting Harris into the play. I had put many Higginses into *My Fair Lady*, and *Camelot* was no problem. We discussed a schedule and a date for Mr. B's exit. A date was indeed set, Mr. Harris proved a quick study, and the exchange was made very seamlessly. It was a full company tearful departure scene when Richard Burton played his last King Arthur, as he was dearly loved by one and all. Richard Harris went in the following night and I, having done my all, also left. The show was in the professional hands of Jonathan Weiss, and so back to New York and the pressures of LFOW (looking for other work)!

I hadn't looked for work very long when I met Peter Neufeld, the general manager of *Annie*, a big hit playing at the Uris Theatre. Peter had me in mind but thought I was away with *Camelot*. His production manager, Janet Beroz, was going to take a three-month leave of absence and would I cover for her? It was a very easy time, the show was running along and selling out. I paid the most attention to the girls playing the orphans, as they had a short attention span and needed a minder every now and then. Jane was back in five weeks and happily so, because I was being offered a new musical called *The Little Prince and the Aviator*, based on the popular book written by Antoine de Saint-Exupéry. It had a book by Hugh Wheeler, a British novelist, dramatist, translator, and poet, who would go on to write *Sweeney Todd*. The show, starring Michael York, was slated to go in three weeks due to Mr. York's commitments. Since I had earned my Director's Guild membership card on the Tony's, I figured I could fill the time stage managing some soap operas around town. I interviewed with Jill Phelps, the producer of *Search for Tomorrow*, who was very helpful. There were not any openings on the show, but there were turnovers all the time and she promised to call me if an opening came up. They allowed me to watch that day to learn the ropes.

The Little Prince and the Aviator, in musical form, was a thin tale of a young prince who travels the planets, addressing themes of friendship and loneliness. It needed a special hand at the helm, being part fairytale, part musical homily. The production was very lucky to have Michael York, well-known from his work on *Cabaret*, and Anthony Rapp, who would grow up to star in *Rent*. The production was being directed by Milton Moss, a stranger to me, and the designer was Eugene Lee, who made our first mistake. Instead of creating a light, effervescent atmosphere in which to tell this fairytale, he plopped a vintage airplane in the middle of the stage surrounding it with a cyclorama painted with clouds. It brought everything down to Earth where I thought it shouldn't be. It was a painful, argument-filled rehearsal period from day one. I tried to be a friendly voice amid the chaos to no avail. As always happens with shows in trouble, management either fires the wardrobe mistress or the director. They fired the director just as we were beginning previews, and with Michael York's insistence, they asked me to replace him. I've done a lot of stupid things in my life; this was at the top of the list. There wasn't much that could be done but calm the two leading players and give Billy Wilson, our very talented choreographer, some time to restage the few musical numbers we had while I made cuts to the banality of the book. We had little time and, no matter where we turned, the damned airplane just stood there eating up space.

We were in the midst of previews, having done two weeks, and the production was beginning to make sense when reality struck. I had arrived at the theater that day in the middle of January to find the stage door closed. Even the box office and the front of the place were abandoned. Our producer, Joseph Tandet, was in some sort of financial difficulties with the Nederlander Theatre Organization and they pulled the plug on Mr. Tandet, closed the show, and threw away the key. We were all standing around at the stage door when Julie Foster, from the office, arrived and gave us the bad news: the Little Prince will never fly again.

Thanks to the rift between Mr. Tandet and the Nederlanders we were all left out in the cold, literally. It was January 15, 1982, just in time for nothing. There were no works going into production until spring. Normally, I would be either in production during the winter lull or preparing a new work for a late spring opening. Anything like that was already set, staff wise. So, I turned to television, what else was there? I grabbed an opening on *Search for*

Tomorrow, my favorite soap-opera because it was produced across the street from Zabar's, my favorite delicatessen. The show had been on the air since 1951 and the stars, Mary Stuart and Larry Haines, were still in their right minds when I joined up. Of all the jobs in show business, the soap opera grind is by far the most difficult, time consuming, pressurized, and nonsensical role to be had. For a play you rehearse at least three weeks before performing; in television you learn a scene at a time, sometimes two or three pages a day; in movies you do no more than half a page a day. But a role in a soap requires you to learn sections of a forty-page script which is then tape recorded and completed that same day. And you do it five days a week, fifty-two weeks a year. An almost impossible task that requires a total commitment to the duty of memorization, and the protection of your sanity. My schedule, however, required no memory and little talent. We met at 7 a.m. for a quick blocking of the day's shoot. By blocking, I mean the action of moving on a certain line of dialogue. Each scene was loosely laid out on the floor of the rehearsal room with chairs, and I would mark my script for the entrance cues I would be giving to actors that day. Taping would begin by 9 a.m. and continue until 7 or 8 p.m., making for a twelve- or thirteen-hour workday, each day.

Attention! Ira Bernstein, Broadway general manager, calling! I prayed this would give me release from TV drudgery. It did; an all-African American cast version of *Guys and Dolls* was being produced, and my name was on the list. Ira, an old friend, was ready to push for me if I was available. I told Ira I would love to do it, that I was available, and if they could get Leslie Uggams, I was in. Two days later, the call came—not only did they have Ms. Uggams to play Sarah, but they also had Richard Roundtree to play Sky, and by the way, I had my offer. I took a leave from *Search for Tomorrow* and began auditions. I ended up with a wonderful cast: Maurice

Hines (Gregory's brother) and a new-comer, Debbie Allen, in her first role on Broadway, as Adelaide. The four leads were fabulous, with great chemistry, and the production was thrilling. The production was never reviewed but played their scheduled two weeks at the Broadway Theatre and went on a long and happy run.

After that fantastic production, I was back to TV. The same facility where *Search from Tomorrow* was normally shot was being used for a pilot episode of *Love, Sidney* starring Tony Randall. It was an easy gig, as Mr. Randall was a quiet professional, and the pilot was done in a week while *Search for Tomorrow* was on hiatus. I prayed for release, and sucker that I am, my old pal Jay Broad offered me some relief. He was in rehearsals with a musical called *Play Me a Country Song* for which he had written the book to a score by John Briggs and Harry Manfredini, of whom I had never heard. They were due to open in ten days and were in the process of firing the director, who I had also never heard of, and still can't remember his name. *Would* I, *could* I? I'm telling you I cannot resist the call. Do I think I have some magic baton to wave, and all will come out fine? Of course not, but besides the sane thought of dropping the phone and running for the hills, I just said "Okay, when do we start?" There was no way to save this show. I let Margo Sappington, a very talented choreographer, break the cast loose and get some movement in the thing while I worked with Jay on the book.

A quick diversion: I had directed a play by Jay Broad called, *A Conflict of Interest*, which we did at the Arena Stage in Washington, DC, a perfect place for the play which dealt with politics. Before rehearsals began, Zelda Fichandler, the dean of the company, arranged for my scene designer, me, and the leading player, Richard Conte, to be escorted to the Cabinet Room in the White House where our play was set. While there, our escort from the Press

Secretary's office got word that President Nixon was leaving for the day, allowing us to sneak a peek at the Oval Office right next door. As we were gawking around, I could see Nixon down the hallway, stop and turn back. We all kind of froze, like kids caught with their hands in the cookie jar, just as he walked in. One of his favorite actors was Richard Conte; they embraced, and we all shook hands. It came to me, knowing my feelings toward Richard Nixon and seeing only two Secret Service men at the door, that I could have whacked the president over the head with my umbrella which no one had confiscated. But I didn't, because when you're in the presence of such important people, no matter who, you stand there smiling like a goon.

Now, back to the mess on hand. Jay and I worked on a plot that was workable and clear enough to put into the show quickly, which we did. Margo cleaned up the dancing and we opened to some of the worst reviews I have ever read. Our first mistake was made when we let the curtain up. I think I put musical theater back some ten years. Who do you think they listed in the program as director? Me, the patsy. Strike three. Bye, Bye Broadway.

Richard Burton & Christine Ebersole in Camelot. *Photo courtesy of Playbill*

7

George Clooney. Robin Wright. George C. Scott. Scott Bakula.

My old pal, Jonathan Weiss, met me at LAX with a copy of the *LA Times* real estate section in hand. and we went directly to a couple of listings. I found a great place in Burbank and rented it. Since you can't go around Los Angeles without a car, I bought a used Jeep, furnished my apartment from a rental company, unpacked, and sat there, with nowhere and nothing to do. Unlike New York, where you can wander the theater district and network, Los Angeles is so spread out that you have to make appointments or wait for calls to get employment. The only people I knew in town were Leon Shamroy, Mary Anderson's husband from the *Lunatics and Lovers* days, Jonathan, and Clark Gable.

Unbeknownst to me, someone from *Search for Tomorrow*, in a chat with a producer on *The Facts of Life*, mentioned me and I got a call. There was an opening on the staff for an air day stage manager and I had an appointment for an interview. The next day, using my new map of Los Angeles County, I struggled to find the NBC Studios which could have been in Omaha for all I knew. I made it in miraculous time.

As an apprentice in network television, I soon learned a quick fact: an air day stage manager worked the two days prior to taping for up-stage cuing and general cast control. Management invented the two-day rule to save money because if you work three days or more you get a full week's wages. Part time work is better than no work, so we mutually agreed to make *The Facts of Life* my first job in California. The show was a successful sitcom on NBC from 1979 until it ended in 1988. It was about a genial housemother, played by Charlotte Rae, who had to mind a group of rich, spoiled young women at an all-girls boarding school. An addition to the regular cast was played by George Clooney, who was destined for better things. The girls on the show were a gaggle of ego monsters, noisemakers, and general trouble. They were the stars of the show, and that early fame was what made the situation understandable. If you grow up with everyone telling you how wonderful, beautiful, and smart you are, you begin to believe it, and everyone else pays the price. The rest of the cast included Cloris Leachman and Molly Ringwald. Clooney had a used convertible, so the two of us were designated carhops at lunch break. Charlotte loved cheeseburgers, so I drove around and filled orders. Filling requests and delivering food was the one thing I loathed, because I'm lousy at math and ultimately ended up paying most of the bills personally. That activity made a big dent in the day's actual work. By Thursday, I quickly learned my cues and spent a good deal of the day rounding up the girls, all four of them, and somehow getting them on set. Friday was a carbon copy of Thursday except, of course, we were taping the show which took a full day.

It was mindless, slightly boring work which made the meager

salary attached to it a nonstarter. I put up with it for almost two months when help came from out of the blue. Jill Farren Phelps, who I had worked for in New York on *Search for Tomorrow* was now executive producer on a NBC soap opera called *Santa Barbara*, a hugely successful show. Ms. Phelps was becoming my personal savior, hiring me wherever I went it seemed. She had an opening for a full-time stage manager which meant a real salary and benefits. When could I start? Would right now be alright?

The studio was in the new NBC production center three blocks from my apartment. I was probably the only person in Burbank who could and would walk to work. The schedule being a duplicate of my New York routine, I could generally be home by 7 p.m., all by the old-fashioned way: walking. The scenario of *Santa Barbara* was simple: three fictitious families lorded over a fictitious town and the rivalry and shenanigans between them made for a tale that had lasted from 1984 until I joined the intrigues, and ultimately spanned ten seasons. There was the Capwell family, played by Jed Alan, Judith McConnell, Robin Wright, Lane Davies, and Nancy Grahn. And the Lockridge family, headed by Louise Sorel and Nicolas Coster. Then there were the more modest Andrade and Perkins families. Eden Capwell, played by Marcy Walker, was involved in an affair with Cruz Castillo, played by A Martinez, which constituted the show's main supercouple and was a source of seemingly endless intrigue. The Capwells and the Lockridges were always striving for attention and were quite fun to watch.

The schedule was the same as the New York show in terms of time, but the day's breakdown was different: after morning blocking, the cast of the day's show would go through a dress rehearsal of sorts, which ended with notes from the producer. This was followed by lunch and finally the taping of the entire episode. There were two stage managers; me and Rob Schiller, who was biding his time until he broke out into a career as a highly successful sitcom director. There was also a standby stage manager, Joe Lumer, who was on tap to cover Rob and me, which gave me the freedom to come and go as I pleased for other engagements.

As it happened, such an opportunity presented itself almost immediately: Bill Siegler, a friend from New York, was coproducing a sitcom called *Mr. President* starring George C. Scott and he needed a unit production manager. He had scoured the membership, but no one wanted to work in any capacity near Mr. Scott. Bill leaned heavily and promised I would hardly see Scott since the job entailed editing each episode and reporting to Bill and his cohort Ed Weinberger (Ed insisted on being billed "Ed."—in private we all called him "Ed Dot"). George Clooney, after doing a pilot with Ed Dot, stated in a 1996 *Vanity Fair* article that, "he was a man who systematically destroys people and bragged about it. There was a meanness to him that I'd never seen before."[13] This was going to be fun.

My job consisted of observing the taping during the week, editing the episode on Saturday and Sunday, and meeting Ed Dot and Bill on Monday. Those meetings were hideous, as Ed Dot seemed to enjoy snide remarks about the quality of my edition and went out of his way to make as many notes as humanly possible detailing changes he wanted me to make. I simply nodded and went on my way, remembering what Scott was putting the directors and crew through. He hurled insults at staff, wasted time, demeaned the scripts, generally made a monster of himself, and reminded one and all that contractually he was to leave at 5 p.m., no matter what. So, there we all were, between a rock and a hard day's work. Siegler, however, was a gem, proving himself as a great go-between and keeping the ball rolling like a fine producer. At the end of my last

---

13   Conant, Jennet. 1996. "Heartthrob Hotel." *Vanity Fair*, December 1996. https://www. vanityfair.com/news/1996/12/george-clooney-199612.

edit meeting, I stood, threw the script in Ed Dot's face, called him a "miserable son of a bitch," and walked out.

When I got back to *Santa Barbara*, word had gotten around that I had worked on Broadway both as a stage manager and director. Suddenly, my opinion was acknowledged, needed, and sought. It was great fun, and made the day go by easier. However, Rick Benewitz, one of our directors, became offended and, rather than complain to me directly, he arranged a meeting with Paul Rauch, our executive producer at the time. The result of the meeting: I threatened to quit, Mr. Rauch threatened to fire me, and, ultimately, we agreed I should stay away from the actors unless they came directly to me. Rick left the meeting smoking his second pack of cigarettes. It was a mistake, and I should have minded my own business; so, while I found it difficult keeping my director tools to myself, I did.

Brad Hall, Julia Louis-Dreyfus's husband, stopped me one day and asked me if I was an actor. I told him who I was, and he explained he was doing a pilot called *Brooklyn Bridge* and he needed one more character for it. It consisted of four guys playing cards around a table and I wouldn't have more than a couple of lines to learn. The whole thing would be done over the weekend when everyone was available. I agreed, thought it would be interesting, and since my weekend was free, I did it. It was my first acting assignment in what would become a second career. Later, a call came at the studio from Don Bellisario, who was the producer of an NBC series called *Quantum Leap* starring Scott Bakula. He was looking for an older New Yorker and Brad Hall had recommended me. I was on a short break at the time, so I quickly told Mr. Bellisario that I had limited experience as an actor, but he cut me off and said, "Brad thinks you're terrific." I agreed to meet during my lunch break the next day and hung up.

It is at this point that I need to confess what my situation was during this time: at that moment, I was a divorced man with four daughters; Emily was part of the Playwright's Workshop of the Actors Studio in New York, Laura was president of the Casting Society in Los Angeles, Amy was living in Las Vegas, and Alisa was an agent in charge of television at the Paradigm Agency. I thought it was best to discuss what may be an offer to appear in *Quantum Leap*, which was a popular show on NBC. Alisa thought the whole thing was insane but agreed I should keep the appointment. She quietly went through my resume with me, reminding me that, at that point in my life, I had spent forty years behind the scenes of theater and television and had never once mentioned acting, let alone had no acting lessons of which to speak. I went anyway. I met the group, read a page of dialogue they gave me, and got the job. After peals of laughter, Alisa made the deal, with me at *top of show*, which means the highest salary to those not under a regular contract. The job was a gas; Scott played Dr. Sam Beckett, a physicist who leaps through time taking on historical mistakes. In this particular episode, I played Lenny, the father of a cab driver who would have died during a robbery if it wasn't for Sam's intervention. It was a wonderful experience, and I happened to be quite good, even sobbing on cue. When it was over, Scott and I shared a big hug, and I went back to my day job.

The producers at *Santa Barbara* were getting a little antsy with my coming and going but I assured them my absences would be minimal in the future. I returned to the cast and my job of cuing and managing the floor with my partner, Rob Schiller. Joe Lumer wasn't as pleased to have me back since he made money whenever I was gone. The cast was astonished when I returned, having done such an important show as *Quantum Leap*. The one desire of daytime actors is to graduate into nighttime, but they stay too long in the barn; the lure of money and security in this cruel business, the fame, as fleeting as it is, and the fear of not making it in the big time weigh heavily on one's conscience. I urged a few to dare knowing they had the talent to try. For example, I thought Louise Sorel had the means to be a fine soubrette in film, like Kay Kendall, Rex Harrison's late wife, who was a uniquely beautiful and funny actress. This rare combination was perhaps best personified by the stunning Carole Lombard. Nancy Grahn and Marcy Walker were both very good dramatic performers, but there they were, bravely toiling away in the barn.

Welcome to West Coast Television. Photo by Alisa Adler

Joe Pesci. Paul Reiser. Helen Hunt. Peter Tolan. Joanna Kerns.

Donna Isaacson, my old friend from New York and head of casting at 20th Century Fox, called to see if I could show her husband, Ken Frankel, around the normal workday of *Santa Barbara*. He was a television director and curious about the inner workings of a soap. I showed him around the next day, and he left that afternoon, shaking his head and vowing never to be curious again. A couple of days later, Donna called to thank me for the courtesy and, in passing, said the director of the movie she was working on kept describing me as one of the characters he wanted. We laughed, I told her how much I enjoyed *Quantum Leap*, and that was the extent of it. The very next day, Donna showed a dub of *Quantum Leap* to the director, and he agreed that he did, in fact, have someone like me in mind. In spite of my misgivings, she graciously sent over the sides, brief portions of the script that actors audition with, which, in this case, were merely a paragraph.

We arranged to meet during my lunch hour. The writer/director was a warm, genial guy named Howard Franklin, who sized me up, chatted about the strangeness of the *Quantum Leap* piece, and let me read the sides twice. We then shook hands, and I rushed back to work. Rob had covered for my lateness and the whole thing was forgotten. Not so fast! Donna's assistant called that evening. She explained that the movie was *The Public Eye* starring Joe Pesci and Barbara Hershey. I had passed the first audition and was scheduled to read with Mr. Pesci and Mr. Franklin. Mr. Pesci was returning from a golf tournament on Saturday after which we would meet at the office. I was early that Saturday for the two o'clock audition, which gave me a chance to read the whole script. Incredibly, this was no small part, it was the third billing after Mr. Pesci and Ms. Hershey. *What are they nuts?* This role called for an established character actor of some experience. No matter, Joe Pesci bounced in and feigned a punch to my solar plexus. It was like old friends as the group formed up. We read most of the script, Mr. Franklin asking for some different emphasis here and there, and finally Mr. Pesci said, "this guy can do any part including mine." He gave me a hug and dashed out. Donna was happily hysterical and called Alisa, who decided to formalize my relationship with the Paradigm Agency.

I had an agent, a major part in a feature film, and a dilemma. *What should I do? Do the movie and probably lose my day job? Collect Social Security and my pensions, and forget the whole thing?* I knew it would be impossible to sit around as a pensioner, clipping coupons and taking a dip in the pool. My daughter, Alisa the agent, thought it would be fun for me and a great way to finish a rather long career by ending it in a movie. I agreed, thanked Donna for an incredible piece of casting, and took another leave from my other vocation.

They picked me up in a stretch limousine and flew me first class to St. Louis where *The Public Eye* was in production. So far this was a lovely deal. The hotel was comfy, and I settled in waiting on word as to when my first day in the movies would begin. Two days later I was still waiting. *Did they forget me? Did they have a change of mind and I'm out of here? I should have brought something to read.* At breakfast on the third day, the desk had a package for me. It was a lot of terrific stuff: lists of staff, cast schedules, and a contract to sign. It also informed me of my first call. The call put me on a set in the midst of being constructed and had me do what must have been a screen test. If it was, they sure brought me a long way for a test, and if it wasn't, what was *this*? Howard Franklin directed a little dialogue from a future scene, with me sitting at a table. In the middle of construction noise and activity, he quieted everyone, rolled camera, and cued me for dialogue. It seemed like a crazy situation, but I did it. After a short break, the first assistant director told me my next call was at 3 a.m. at an outdoor location and mentioned it was number thirty-one in my script, which was waiting for me at the hotel. Kindly, he told me to get some rest, as it would be a long night. Rest, hell, I've been locked up in my room for nearly seventy-two hours. This gave me time to read the whole script again and I was amazed at the extent of my part.

About two that afternoon, that same AD called to say I would be picked up at 1 a.m. for costume fittings and make-up. I was on my way at one in the morning and went through a horrendous costume session as soon as I arrived. This jacket could go with this shirt, that suit goes well with these shirts and ties, the shoes must fit, the whole thing was endless, trying on pants and jackets, shoes, and coats. They then sent me to the make-up van which, happily, took no time. The shoot was simple: Mr. Pesci (I was then told to call him "Joe") was exiting what was supposed to be a hospital, having just recovered from a gunshot wound and I, along with a policeman, was meeting him and escorting him to a waiting car. There were many reporters yelling at us and a crowd of onlookers shoving and pushing so as to hinder Joe and me from getting away as fast as possible. I had no written dialogue, just attempts at getting through the crowd. We did that scene a number of times, with the camera at different positions, and as dawn began breaking, the shoot was over.

I was gassed, and by the time I got back to the hotel, all I could do was fall into a big, cushy armchair and pull myself together. I hadn't fallen asleep, I don't think, when an envelope slid under the door, right in front of me. *I'm gone, am I not?* Canned after the first day! *Was I that bad?* I thought I handled the crowd pretty well. *Did I push Joe, or hold his arm too tightly?* How embarrassing now to crawl back to *Santa Barbara*, a total failure. I hadn't the strength to get up and open the damned thing, but my curiosity got the better of me; I had to see what reasons were given for the disaster. I stumbled over, picked it up, leaned on the door and read the contents. It was my call for the next day of filming.

Having observed scores of actors at work, even directing many of them myself, I soon put into practice what my experience told me each scene was really about at its core. How would I direct this scene if I was directing it? I listened, most important of all, I listened. The whole experience was unique. The atmosphere was new and the energy one needed to keep the scenes fresh in spite of the delays made it a challenge. In the end, I learned a lot. I think I gave a good performance, and I enjoyed it so much that I looked for more. On the last day on the film, I asked Howard why he had obviously flinched when we first met back in Burbank. Apparently, he had said to himself as we shook hands, "Oh God, I hope he can act!" By the way, I was right; what I thought must have been a screen test was actually even more. Howard said it was a little test to see if my nerves were capable of holding up amidst a difficult atmosphere and see if all that newness and disjointed focus would throw me. *Interesting.*

Matt Kaplan, a congenial, affable, and most organized gentleman, was assigned by Paradigm to be my contact. We became quite phone friendly very quickly upon my return to Burbank from Chicago, where filming for *The Public Eye* ended up. Alisa called, as *The Public Eye* needed me on Sunday for "ADR." Sunday, as it happened, was the only day available. I was ecstatic, assuming it was a company screening of the movie, which I had not seen, not for a moment. The address was the same as when I first met Howard Franklin, millenniums ago. The guard at the gate gave me a map of the lot and pointed to B-133. Off I went. I knocked expectantly but heard no reply, so I went in. The door closed behind me, leaving me in total darkness. Suddenly, I was in hands-out, feet-frozen in-place, eyes-staring-into-nothingness pitch black. I called out, but there was still no reply. I feebly hunted for the door, considering the all-too-likely possibility of falling on my face—or my ass. I felt the wall, but where was I to go along the wall? Which direction? I had lost all perception of space and distance. I surrendered, and stood there, a hapless zombie.

Suddenly, a voice, "Is that Jerry Adler, two o'clock?"

"Hey, could you turn on a light? I'm in the dark here," I called out.

He replied, "Oh, sorry," not sounding particularly sorry.

A screen lit up, revealing I was in a small theater containing two rows of seats. I assumed he was going to show the movie, but couldn't help but wonder: *Where the hell is everybody?*

"If you're all set, I think we can begin," he said.

"This is just for me?" I queried.

"I wish. We have more later today," he responded.

"I can't understand why you don't get everyone in at one time, but you know better."

"Let's get started. You ready?" He asked.

I plopped down on one of the movie seats, getting comfortable like I would when watching a screener the DGA, Director's Guild of America, sends members at Oscar's voting time.

"Ready and waiting," I said.

The screen came alive and there I was with Pesci and the policeman, pushing our way through the crowd. Instantly, the screen went dead. *Oh, damn*, I thought to myself, *just my luck, they've got a big problem with the edit."*

"What's the matter?" he asked.

"I don't know. You tell me. The movie started and then died," I answered.

"Did you hear the cue?" he asked.

"What are you talking about? The movie was on for a second and then it went black," I said, growing more confused.

"I'm talking about the cue. Did you hear the cue?" He asked.

"What cue?" I asked, at a loss.

"Come on, man. Is your headset not working?" He asked, growing agitated.

"There's no headset. What headset?" I asked.

"I'll be right out," he said, flatly.

He appeared through a door in the black wall. He was just a kid, and he was pissed seeing me sitting there.

"What the hell are you doing here? You should be up there on the headset!" He said, annoyed.

"Don't be mad. It was bloody dark," I responded.

He pointed to a faintly lit area in the back. There was a music stand with a set of headphones hanging on it and a stool.

"Come on. Stop wasting time and get on the headset," he said, rudely.

He disappeared through an invisible door in the black wall. I ran back and put on the headphones. I could hear him very clearly now.

"Okay, let's get a level," he said.

This part I knew from my days stage managing. But why would they need a countdown to start a movie? This whole thing was getting ridiculous but, like some obedient monkey, I counted.

"Great! Now here we go everybody, we got a first!" He said.

That same scene came and went again. I stood there, helplessly, but I did hear it much better than before.

"Now what? What the hell are you doing?" He asked, angrily.

"In about two minutes, I'm out of here," I lightly warned him. "And pardon the expression, but what the fuck is going on?"

"Well, it's simple. I play the bit. You hear the cue. You read the dialogue on the paper sitting on the music stand in front of you. That's the way it's been since the day you were born," he said, arrogantly.

I didn't enjoy the sarcasm, but I was obviously in uncharted waters. I apologized and offered my complete attention. The apology must have been accepted because he played the scene again.

"You heard it again and did nothing. Why is that, for Christ's sake?" He asked, reaching a pinnacle of rudeness.

"I am going to say this one more time, before I ram this headset down your throat. I arrived totally new at this, and I mean no harm. You must help, not carry on. I beg you," I said.

He appeared again out of the darkness. He stared at my gray hair and sweating face, and realized I was entirely new to this mumbo jumbo, as crazy as it seemed. He slowly went through the ritual: in the middle of whatever scene was being shown on the screen, there would be a sharp ping at which time I was to lip-sync whatever was coming out of my mouth on screen. Following his explanation, I performed admirably. We successfully lip-synced three words and it was done. Marty, the adolescent engineer, congratulated me and as I started to leave, many lights in the ceiling brightly came on. Great. Dark when you arrive, bright when you leave. As I opened the door, I asked Marty what ADR stood for. He said: "Additional Dialogue Replacement." *Everybody knows that.* I was glad to get home and rest my guilt ridden and embarrassed body. I was so hooked on seeing the movie, I forgot ADR was called *looping* in New York. Learn from your mistakes and move on.

I had promised Rob Schiller, my old partner in crime, that I would cover for him. He was to direct an episode of *Santa Barbara*, so he was on prep week starting Monday. *Prep week* means preparing your camera shots according to the layouts of the scenes involved, checking locations if the script calls for scenes out of the studio, and most importantly, learning where in the action your script lies. Soaps are not done in consecutive action, it does its best to do so, but many incidents betray that; actor availability, scenery construction clogging the stage floor, script changes, and so on. Sometimes your work on a show includes scenes out of order, leaving you ignorant of the action of the day. You would need a session with the producers to explain where you are in the *bible,* the road map.

I checked on Rob then started for bed when the phone rang, "Hold for Mr. Pollock," a voice said, as soon as I picked up. I waited, as hold music began.

After a moment, Mr. Pollock, whoever he was, picked up, "Hey, Jerry, you are terrific. I saw the picture as soon as I got off the plane and you killed it. Really."

This guy must be somebody, with a secretary and a plane, but who was he?

I thanked him and added, "How was it? I haven't seen it, you know. How did you get a copy?"

Mr. Pollock laughed so loud he coughed then hung up.

It bothered me all night. He probably was one of our producers and I made a bad impression. I called Rob to see if he knew the mysterious Mr. Pollock, but Rob had turned in. The next morning at *Santa Barbara*, I went to Louise Sorel, as she knew everyone and everything.

"Lou, can I ask you something? A guy called me late last night and I have no idea who the hell he is."

Louise quickly asked, "How did he get your number? What did he want?"

She was right. How did he get my number? I wasn't listed anywhere. Maybe he was one of our producers, after all.

"I don't know, Lou, it was damned late. The phone rang, and before I could say 'Hello' a voice said, 'Hold for Mr. Pollock.'"

Louise quickly said, "You sure it was Pollock?"

I was sure. "And, he said he saw the picture and I killed it. He got a copy and liked it, whoever he is," I added.

Louise kind of whispered, "I know who he is, he's chairman of Universal Pictures. Your boss."

Good Lord. I may never work again.

Afterwards, recovering from my major faux pas, I logged ten auditions that Matt Kaplan booked for me, including a reading for a part in *The Fresh Prince of Bel Air*. Nine of the auditions were failures, but I realized during this period that I enjoyed auditioning, meeting people, giving a good read, and waiting for a hopefully good reaction. This business is worse than baseball; one for ten is slightly below average but keeps you in the game. My one out of ten ended up being one of the most important auditions I ever had; I read for a part on *Mad About You* and got it. The episode was great fun. I was a policeman at the precinct when Helen Hunt and Paul Reiser arrive, frantically looking for their dog. The show came off exceedingly well and I enjoyed being with them and, luckily, they thought I was terrific. This episodic stuff was a gas. After that, I immediately booked a pilot called *Sluggers* where I played a kind of Tommy LaSorda character with a Little League baseball team. Pilots take a week to do, with many changes along the way and an audience watching the final performance. It was my first audience participation and I loved it. The show didn't get picked up, however, meaning "thank you, but no thanks."

Soon after, things got serious. I read for two movies, *Carlito's Way*, starring Sean Penn and Al Pacino (not bad) and *Wolf* starring Jack Nicholson (also not bad). I didn't get either one, but it was weird auditioning for Mike Nichols, who was directing *Wolf*. We hugged upon seeing each other. He didn't make me read the sides and said: "Give me your number. When I need an old Jew, I'll call you." Sadly, I never met him again. What a major loss that was, losing him at such a young age.

Next came one of my favorite jobs. I read for this pilot and hit a homer. It was the funniest script I had read since I started this auditioning business. It was called *The Long Game* and revolved around a female professional golf player hampered by living with her grandfather temporarily. It starred Joanna Kerns, Margo Martingdale as Joanna's character's agent, and me. The terrific Phil Leeds was also in the cast. Phil had been blacklisted during the McCarthy debacle and lost a lot of work during his best years. We did the pilot, and it was hilarious, but the networks passed because it was felt that the basic premise was too new for the general public. Just like our writer/director, Peter Tolan, to be way ahead of everyone. The show was about the world of female golfers in 1993, but with the long overdue respect for and interest in women's sports nowadays, *The Long Game* would be a hit. The audience during the taping of the show loved it. Nobody knows a hit even when it stares them right in the eye. After that, I auditioned for a few lackluster, and for the most part, silly shows. One of them was probably likely to get picked up and be a big hit, who knew—maybe Norman Lear or Carl Reiner did, but they were too smart to run a network.

My first day as a motion picture actor with Joe Pesci. Original photo by Universal Pictures—© 1992

Nightclub scene from Public Eye. *Photo courtesy of Universal Studios Licensing LLC*

Mr. Wicker on Mad About You *with Paul Reiser & Helen Hunt.*
Photo credit: MAD ABOUT YOU. © 1992, 1993 *TriStar Television,*
Inc. All Rights Reserved. Courtesy of Sony Pictures Television

9 | Woody Allen. Rob Morrow.
Diane Keaton.

Alisa called, sounding a little mutedly excited. "How would you like to audition for Woody Allen?" She asked.

A quick question was quickly answered. "That would be a blast," I responded. "Who do I have to kill?"

She had gotten a call from Juliet Taylor, a top casting director, notifying her that Woody Allen was working on a new movie, and that he would like me to come in and meet him. *Would like to meet me? Where the hell does that come from? How does he even know who I am?* Alisa figured he must have seen me in something. What? *The Public Eye? Probably, because what else is there?* Whatever it was, I jumped at the chance and agreed to fly to New York and meet him. Anytime.

I flew to New York a day early, just to be up and ready. I stayed at my brother Mike's apartment, and he and his wife, Marlene, were more nervous than I was. I stayed awake half the night. The agency called bright and early, as my meeting was set for one o'clock in Mr. Allen's office. I had hoped for an earlier call, but I was doomed to sit around all morning with Mike assuring me that Woody would be lucky to have me. Lucky or not, I presented myself at the proper address, which was a fancy apartment house on upper Park Avenue. You practically had to have a Visa to get past the doormen. Finally, Ms. Taylor greeted me in the lobby, and we went in, robbing the doorman of a chance to throw me out. We entered a vestibule or anteroom with a small couch and chair. Ms. Taylor asked me to sit and let me know that Woody would be right with me. She left through the only other door, and I waited. What seemed like hours was broken when Ms. Taylor came back and handed me a pack of papers. She told me to look them over and disappeared. These were no sides, they looked like half of the movie. There were five separate scenes, each clipped alone. If I hadn't been a fast reader, this pile of stuff could have taken a couple of hours to get through. The character's name was Paul, he was a neighbor down the hall. The scenes were innocuous, simple chat except for the last one. It was a menace of some sort. I read it aloud in this empty hole-in-the-wall as any actor would and tried to figure out what he saw in me and how I could make an impression without knowing a damn thing of what he was looking for. The spell was broken by Ms. Taylor who gave me the ground rules: "Don't attempt to shake hands or greet him in any way, he's very shy. Just give your name and wait for instructions." I was shown that each scene was in order, but I probably wouldn't do all of them, and she added that she would read all the other parts with me. So far, all of this promised to keep me totally off balance.

We entered what must have been the living room of the apartment. Did he live here? We stood in an area that was fully lit while everything else was shadowed in darkness. Here I go again, dark into light. Juliet announced me and jerky me, I said, "Yes, Jerry

Adler. Hi." Not a word. I didn't even know where he was, as the rest of the room was really dim. After a time, his head appeared over the back of the couch by the shaded window. Not his whole head, but just enough to look me over.

"Would you do the first piece?" Woody asked.

Juliet and I read together. At least, I was better than she was. Silence. Awkward silence.

"Read the next one. It's one page," Woody called out.

"The one where I meet him and his wife outside the building?" I questioned.

Silence. I began to think I was auditioning in a mausoleum.

"Are they marked?" I asked.

"Yes. Please read number three," replied Woody.

That was a tough one. In the scene, the three of us: Woody, Mia Farrow (his real partner, at the time, was playing his movie wife), and I were together in his apartment where we were studying his stamp collection. My character was a collector too. It was neighborly chat mostly about stamps. I guess it was going to be a comedy scene in the movie, because all the foreign stamps were in a language that would invite laughter. In a movie, yes. In an audition, ludicrous tongue-twisting was all that could be mustered. It really wasn't fair trying to fake these names in a scene I had just read once. I screwed it up, *royally*. Maybe that's what he wanted. Does this guy have a sense of humor? Whatever the test, he sure didn't laugh, neither did Juliet. I think for anyone to do that scene well in an audition, they'd have to be a comic genius.

"The fourth is easier. Read that one, please," said Woody, from somewhere in the darkness.

Another one? I think I had read the entire movie already. I was getting ready to stagger to a chair, when the little head bobbed up and I think I saw his face.

"I know it's difficult. But it's important. Number five will give you a chance to let it all out. Number five, please," said Woody.

Number five was meant to antagonize total hostility towards a person and, cleverly, he set me up in that last scene. I really tore it up. The scene ended, a perfectly performed reading. *Silence.*

Finally, Woody said, "Thank you. Ms. Taylor will see you out."

She did. We stopped in the anteroom, where she exclaimed how much he loved me.

"What makes you say that?" I asked.

"He spoke to you! He let you read all the pages," Juliet replied.

I was impressed with myself. She told me to wait a minute and went into His Majesty's Lair. I really got a kick out of all this, flying here for what I thought was just a tryout and making an impression. Wait till I tell Alisa, I thought. After a few moments, Juliet returned, thanked me, and asked where I was staying. I explained I was staying with my brother and would go home sooner than later.

"Give me his number and if anything comes up, I'll call you. You were terrific. Thanks for coming," said Juliet.

By the time I got to Mike's apartment, I was dreaming of an Oscar. Mike and I relived the audition, and he instilled a brotherly sense of reality. Clearly, he brought me down for a soft landing. We realized there must have been dozens of actors experiencing the same reaction as I did. God knows how anyone actually gets cast.

Well, the phone rang early that evening. Ms. Taylor thanked me again and asked if I would still be in New York the next day.

"If it's for the show, I can stay as long as it takes," I offered.

Juliet then told me that I was needed for costume fittings in the morning and gave me all the details. Can you imagine? As crazy as it seems, I got the job. Even Mike was hysterical. Wait till I call Alisa, my actual agent now, that I landed the part. Indeed, she was amazed and told me to do the fittings and get back quickly.

It is completely difficult to relate how nutty the whole thing was, standing there in my underwear with this tailor fussing with me. I couldn't help tooting my own horn a little, telling him one of the most miraculous stories in the annals of show business lore.

"You're talking about the Woody Allen picture, aren't you? Don't buy the convertible yet. They send everyone from the West Coast for fittings here because they're too cheap to fly you back for this if you actually get the job," said the tailor.

I couldn't wait to get my clothes on and get the hell out of there. What a putz I was, boasting all around this dingy place like a colossal schmuck. Before I flew back, I had a wonderful lunch at Barney Greengrass. They make the best eggs and onions in the world, which sounds horrible but is surprisingly delicious. I called Mike to cluck about reality and made a mad dash for the airport; in those days, you could get there, wait in line, and get on a plane within forty-five minutes. As I flew back to Los Angeles, I had one regret: I didn't shop at Zabar's before I left.

It was a pretty somber meeting at the Paradigm office the next morning, as Alisa had already checked with Juliet Taylor's people and was told that I was still "in the loop," whatever that meant. So, the tailor was right. They fit everyone who is in the loop. At least I was in the loop after all that sweat and toil. At least Matt Kaplan joined us with good news: while I was gone, *Mad About You* had called with an offer; they wanted me to be a recurring character on the following season. I had money stashed away from my *The Public Eye* days, so I really wasn't ready to jump at the chance. What would happen if I accepted *Mad About You* and Woody came through? I forgot for that moment that I was sitting in a stronghold. It's generally advantageous to take the first offer, and if the second one arrives, it can always be dealt with. It was my first offer to join a popular show like *Mad About You* as a recurring character, and

I had previously had a terrific time playing the cop on the show. How nice that they had remembered me. *What the hell, a cop can be funny, I was in.* Their season had already begun, so I waited to be called in. Just then I got another offer. Jeez, I must have been the busiest guy in America! It was a show called *Northern Exposure*, which was being shot in Canada. The offer was a few weeks away, so I stalled them, and checked in with *Mad About You.* They wanted to cast me as the super of a building. I reminded them that I was a cop before. Their answer, "Nobody will remember." And so, I did my first show as the super on *Mad About You*, and they were friendly and welcoming. Paul Reiser and Helen Hunt are at the top of my list if I had one. I discussed my other problem with management, and they okayed my doing *Northern Exposure* during the off-week. All shows had the same schedule: three weeks of production and one week off. Our off week was in two weeks and *Northern Exposure* approved the dates. By the way, nobody remembered me as the cop—except Paul.

As it turned out, *Northern Exposure* was not produced in Canada, but in a tiny town near Redmond, Washington, and was a stand-in for the fictional location of the show, Cicely, Alaska. The star of the show was Rob Morrow, who played Dr. Joel Fleischman, stuck in Cicely to pay off his medical loans. In the episode, he was fantasizing about his future while lazily rowing in a canoe on the lake in town. I played Rabbi Shulman who rises out of the waters and, soaking wet, delivers a kind of "Sermon on the Fountain." It was a wonderful, witty, and humorous script. The only problem was getting me to rise from the lake, join him in the boat, and play the scene without drowning. They constructed a huge, plastic covered pool on the local high school basketball court. This one was a monster, almost four feet deep, and supported all around somehow without destroying the arena. They then filled it slowly to detect any leaks. I was duly impressed and wondered what would happen when all two hundred pounds of me was submerged like some dead whale floating about. I needed not worry; I was replaced by a crash dummy who could probably play the scene better than me. We rehearsed on dry land for a while and Rob was very kind, knowing what I had gotten myself into. I warned everyone that I wasn't happy to do a lot of takes; one or two submarines and I was out of there. The idea was that I would go under the water and crouch, holding my breath until an assistant director in a snorkel would tap my leg as the cue. On top of all of this, I would be wearing a black suit, shirt, and tie and, of course, black shoes. I think even Seabees would demur. So, what could I do? Quit and let them find some other crazy rabbi? I was stuck. They had me climb up the ladder, reach out to another ladder, and climb down into the phony lake. The water was warm, thank goodness, and so, I stood there up to my waist, waiting while they shot the rest of the scene. Rob slowly came to a spot, then suddenly reacted to something. The camera moved to another location, lights were adjusted and, with Rob's admiration, down I went. It was so weird, crouching, fully dressed in the water and, after what seemed eternity, I got the cue. Up I went, and I grabbed hold of the other end of the canoe. We had never fully rehearsed climbing into the canoe, not to mention, while soaking wet. Instantly, like the trooper I was, I threw my legs into the boat and dragged myself in. Rob was happily surprised. There I was, dripping while playing the scene. It went perfectly with great applause from the crew. With God's help, we didn't have to do it again. I hugged Rob, shook hands with everyone, and went to bed to dry off. In the morning, I had breakfast in the little motel we were in. The menu listed "Larks and Eggs." I settled for toast and coffee and got out of town.

It was quiet for a while. I spent my time auditioning for pilots, most of which never got produced. It's crazy, you audition for a pilot, you're happy for a while, and then they don't do the pilot. Worse yet, you do the pilot, and then the network doesn't pick it up. I did nine in a row, three of which I passed on for fear I would get the part and I would be stuck in some terrible show that gets picked up. Crazy. I did audition for a movie with Jodie Foster in which she plays a girl who had spent her life in the jungle, kind of like Tarzan. The audition was a classic, reading the pages with a casting person uttering the jungle dialogue. I'd read a line and the casting person would go, "hand hoodie any," then it'd be my turn again, followed by another "hoot hatter hoo," from the casting person. This went on for a while before I quit. Anyway, *Northern Exposure* called. I told Matt Kaplan to get assurance that the episode took place on dry land. It did. The episode was fun, featuring just Rob and me, wandering around different cities, discussing his future decisions. I was a bit like that character out of the old movie *Here Comes Mr. Jordan,* wherein Rob could see me but no one else could. At one point, they had constructed the side of a New York subway car for a very long scene. This one took four days and I enjoyed all of them.

Well, what do you know? That champion of agents, Alisa, my first-born daughter, the person most guarding my career, called: "You got it. You got the part in Woody Allen's movie."

How do you like that? I had kind of written the whole thing off.

"My God! What happens next? I don't need to go back for fittings, they have them. See how clever they are?" I mused, happily.

I was to wait for a start date which would come in a few days or weeks while Alisa made the deal. The whole thing was very exciting and waiting to hear from New York was excruciating. To while away the time, I covered the guys at *Santa Barbara,* and dreamt of movie making. The weeks turned into months when suddenly the scandal hit the papers: Mia Farrow was accusing Woody of inappropriate behavior with their children, and now we knew what the delay was all about. The media loves a juicy scandal and this one was a beaut. The next shock came quickly; Mia was out of the movie and casting was going forward. Soon the Woody Allen and Mia Farrow debacle reached the courts, and the tentative starting date on the movie was postponed. I figured that was the death knell on the picture. There was a lot of ugly stuff being thrown around and soon any word as to the film happening died. At least I had my spasmodic day job to fall back on. Two months later, a judge awarded Mia custody of the younger children, and Woody was free to marry Soon-Yi Previn, one of Mia's adopted brood; but everyone knows all this. The startling news was that Diane Keaton was now starring in the movie. Amazingly, a start date of May 1, 1992, was announced and casting had finished with Angelica Huston, Joy Behar, Ron Rifkin, and Alan Alda, whom I hadn't seen since I stage-managed *The Apple Tree*. I was in heady company. I announced that *Santa Barbara* was to be my last technical job in television come hell or anything else. The cast threw me a great farewell party at the nearby Chinese Dynasty restaurant. Weirdly, my fortune cookie read: "You May Soon Change Your Line of Work." I kid you not, I've saved it all these years.

Deals were done, contracts were signed, and I was off to New York. A grand hotel was arranged for me, and I flopped down in its small living room, ready to go to work. There was a full packet waiting for me, with staff info, contact lists and the scene we were to shoot in forty-eight hours. I even got to learn the title of the movie: *Manhattan Murder Mystery*. I had yet to read the full script and the upcoming scene was like the one I had read at my audition: a meeting in front of our building. The meeting took place in the late afternoon, as my character was returning from food shopping and the others were off to the theater; a friendly, innocuous, and innocent greeting followed by a parting. Certainly not very dramatic but it was either a set-up for some future event or simply old neighbors saying "Hello." Better learn the material and wait for direction.

The pick-up van came right on time, dropped me at the building location of 200 East 78th Street, which had no augmenting lights. A happy associate took me to my dressing room van, a "2-banger" I shared with the cinema photographer, Carlo di Palma. Woody and Diane shared one right across the street. Pretty sumptuous digs for a lowly player. My costumes were hanging in the van, make-up was up the street. I met Diane Keaton for the first time when I entered the hair and make-up van. She jumped up, kissed me on both cheeks, and welcomed me to "The Funny Farm." They did a little touch up on me, and combed my hair, which was still dark in those days. I dressed quickly and waited in my van for a call. Waiting is the notorious evil on movie sets, it could be a technical wait, a diva wait, a director wait, or just wait. Word came that we were waiting for the results of a meeting between Woody and Carlo di Palma as to where to put the scene. It was finally agreed that we would do it in front of the building, as Woody and Diane came out through the front, stopping to greet me coming down the street. The scene went well, Woody disregarding his own rewrites and causing Diane and me to ad lib some.

I did get a bit of direction when Woody took me aside and said, "Not so avuncular. Simple, okay?"

Okay. What's avuncular? He also said *simple*, so that's what I did. We did it three times while di Palma, with a hand-held camera, panned the group on each take. After the third take, Woody yelled "*Cut!*" He chatted with di Palma for a while and said: "Fine. Moving on. Goodnight."

I changed, got dressed, and was driven to the hotel.

* * *

SIDEBAR: It was during this busy but fascinating time that my beloved brother, the family matchmaker, reintroduced me to a woman I had met through his group of friends. When we had first met, she was married but had since divorced. Mike set up a meeting; we met and have been inseparable ever since. It had been my intention not to explore family or personal relationships in this book, but Joan, my wife, has been such an intrinsic part of the events to come, it seems impossible not to include her in the rest of the narrative. I'll mention us as a couple in the future as the situation warrants.

My next call, a few days after the meeting scene, was to take place in the Lipton apartment; Diane and Woody were the Liptons, and I was Paul House. The production had rented the top floor of a building not yet completed and had furnished that area to be where the Liptons and Mr. House lived. Woody's apartment included a living room and kitchen as well as a bedroom area being finished for future scenes. It was an amazement to see what scenic designers and decorators can do to create workable and livable spaces out of nothing. The scene was meant to establish that I was a next-door neighbor who had recently lost his wife to some unknown disease or accident. It was during this time that I found out that Woody suspected me of murdering her. This explains why I was cast in the movie in the first place: if I am really the murderer named in the title, it is brilliant to cast a lesser-known actor in the part. A well-known character actor would immediately give the plot away.

As far as talent was concerned, I asked Robert Greenhut, our producer, how I was doing. His quick answer was: "you're still here, aren't you?" He explained, having worked with Woody for quite a few years, that Woody relies heavily on casting the right person in the right part. If the actor fails to meet his expectations right at the beginning of work, he is quickly replaced. Hence, he relies on casting rather than direction—if you ain't it, you're out!

In the scene, I'm invited in by Woody, so that we can share our respective stamp collections as we're both collectors. Woody shows me his book of stamps, much like the scene I had read in the audition, but with fewer foreign names. Scenes would be added later showing the Liptons trying to find out if my wife exists, had existed, and where she could be now. Funny bits. The scene was a bore without them. What was nice was spending a little off-camera time with Diane, who was probably tired of being questioned about one of my favorites, *The Godfather*, but didn't hesitate to chat about it with me. What interested her more were her collections of clown paintings and stories. She said what we need is more clowns to give us a little humor in our lives. Amen.

The scene went well even though I had no idea what I was talking about. Woody kept turning pages, and I kept admiring the stamps. I was confident the funny scenes of the Liptons' hidden activity in my apartment while I was busy stamp-gazing in theirs, would make the scene work. We did the pages a few times with Mr. di Palma, king of the handheld cameras, panning all over the room. Woody doesn't block any staging for the whole scene, he just set us up at the start and we kind of walked and sat as if in reality. It was easy for me, as I ended up at his desk. This was the first use of the apartments, and it caused quite a snarl in traffic because our production vans were parked on West 79th street from Broadway all the way over to West End Avenue. It was a great location for me to do lunch at a nearby deli, and for friends to drop in on me and chat in my dressing room van. Joan couldn't always make it, as she had a big job with a luggage firm at that time, but she snuck away once in a while. The whole area was my old stomping ground, as I used to live on West 69th, did my first soap opera job on Broadway and 80th, and the Theatre District wasn't too far.

I was really beginning to enjoy myself when Woody decided to rewrite the entire course of the movie; I was no longer a stamp collector, and that long scene about stamps would be gone. I now owned an art house movie theater. At the time he announced this major change, no one knew what he had up his sleeve. I was nearing the end of my contractual days, and the scenes where the Liptons would confront me about the murder of my wife as well as the denouement of the film as written were next on the present agenda. All that was thrown away because Woody had a new ending he was preparing. It meant I needed to stay on at least another week which was very okay with me. I was enjoying New York (especially on per diem), going into overtime, and seeing as much as possible of Joan.

The reason Woody was redoing so much of the script was because, in essence, Paul House backstage at his theater as he hunts the Liptons down was much like the finale in *The Lady from Shanghai*. That Orson Welles movie set its finale in a fun house where his character hunted his enemies down in a sea of mirrors. Woody was going to do his own version backstage at the rented Liberty Theater on West 42nd Street in Manhattan. In the film, I kidnap Diane then bind and gag her in a small dressing room at the Liberty. After I lure Woody there to save Diane, Woody and I get into a chase on stage, hiding behind mirrors while *The Lady from Shanghai* plays on the screen. The combination of real events diametrically reflecting the cinema events on the theater screen was a brilliant idea. Doing it was a terribly time consuming and intricate chore. As in the movie, a trio was involved in the action: Orson Welles, Everett Sloane, and Rita Hayworth. Woody added a woman to create his trio. He couldn't use Diane, as I had her imprisoned up in the room, so he invented Paul's secretary: an older paramour, jealous of Diane, who appears with a gun and, during the melee, shoots Paul. Woody named her Mrs. Dalton and Marge Redmond played her. The damn scene took days, nearly driving me nuts with all the appearing and disappearing behind mirrors and shards of glass. My last day on the film was the scene in which I had to tie up Diane and call Woody on the phone. It was great fun, and we couldn't keep Diane from giggling. I got a great hug from Diane, and Woody said I did a fine job.

Me with *Woody Allen and Diane Keaton* on Manhattan Murder Mystery *as (spoiler alert) the murderer.* Photo credit: MANHATTAN MURDER MYSTERY. © 1993 *TriStar Pictures, Inc. All Rights Reserved. Courtesy of TriStar Pictures*

And me, the murderer, in Paris

Alfred Molina. Sundance Film Festival.

Matt Kaplan suggested I wait for a good offer rather than running around auditioning for everything. The effect of *Manhattan Murder Mystery* was expected to give me a nice push when the movie opened. Meanwhile, I did some more *Northern Exposure* and *Mad About You* episodes. Howard Franklin, the director of *The Public Eye*, my first movie job, asked me to do a cameo scene in a movie he was doing. I would do anything for him, so I played an announcer organizing a group at some sort of convention. I have no idea what the scene meant nor what the movie was about. As a matter of fact, I have no idea if the movie opened to the public, but I loved working with Howard again.

The *Mad About You* people seemed to love the character they invented, the super, Mr. Wicker, and so they filled my work schedule by popping me into the show quite often. I even auditioned for a major pilot called *Everybody Loves Raymond* starring Ray

Romano, who created the show. I read a scene from the script and spent some time chatting with the producers, Phil Rosenthal and Ray Romano himself. It was a very friendly atmosphere, and I had the feeling I was in the running to play Ray's father. We talked about dates and locations so specifically, I left the meeting confidently. Ultimately, they hired Peter Boyle for the part, who was fabulous in the show. So much for feeling confident.

I was doing another episode of *Mad About You* when I got an offer to spend three months in conjunction with the Sundance Film Festival, joining Alfred Molina as professionals reading works by neophyte screenwriters. It was a great gig, giving Joan and me some wonderful time together. She joined me there where they supplied us with a cabin by a river and allowed Joan to ride their horses while Alfred and I read scripts that were submitted to the festival's artistic jurors. It was all very bucolic. I had a great time with Alfred, and I think we did a professional job, out of which came people like Tamara Jenkins, now a noted filmmaker.

Howard Franklin strikes again! He was doing another wacky movie. This one was called *Larger Than Life* and was about a man who has inherited an elephant in his uncle's will and goes on a trip to California where he plans to sell it. The script was full of cameo appearances and Howard had set Bill Murray as the poor guy stuck with an unwanted creature. He also had Matthew McConaughey, Janine Garofalo, Jeremy Piven, and Pat Hingle. What a group. I did a tiny bit in the opening scene and kept my streak alive: I'm in every Howard Franklin movie to date.

Tony Danza. Sam Waterston. Adrien Brody. Debbie Harry. Carol Leifer.

There was a most interesting audition waiting for me when I finished *Larger Than Life*. Tony Danza was doing a pilot titled *Hudson Street*, which was a comedy/drama set in a precinct house about a cop, his ex-wife, young son, and the crime reporter with whom he is having an affair. I loved the two sides I was given. The character I was to read was Lt. Al Teischer, and a date was set to meet the casting people. The building was in West Hollywood and there were no door numbers, only cards denoting the person or show inside. I kept wandering about, knocking on doors, interrupting meetings, and such. I was on my way down and out the front door when I literally bumped into Mr. Danza and the producers, Nat Bernstein and Randi Singer. We laughed about my wandering the building and they promised to hang signs for future auditions. Danza loved *Mad About You*, especially the cop I played on the show. We were still in the lobby as he told me all about the show. My role sounded great. Finally, Danza asked me if I was interested in playing Al, and I kind of jumped at the suggestion. I hadn't read a word of the sides yet. We shook hands all around, Tony gave me a quick hug, and they were gone, leaving me alone in the lobby. Obviously, I do great in lobbies.

By the time I got home, there was a message on my answering machine, *ah, those were the days*: I had the part, and a deal was in the making. That was the way all auditions should go. I learned a lot about the show in the next few days. Besides Tony Danza, the cast included Lori Loughlin, Christine Dunford, and Tom Gallop. The start date was to be in early September 1995. The show was scheduled for twenty-two half-hour episodes, and I had third billing. There was great anticipation concerning the show and the return of Tony Danza to nighttime television. The whole atmosphere led me to believe that I was involved in a major production running many seasons.

It all began ideally; we had our own permanent stage at Sony Studios in Culver City just north of Los Angeles. With a newly constructed two-story dressing room addition at one end of the stage, I could have lived in the room assigned to me. Everything about the production was first-class, from the permanent sets, the spacious costume department built under the dressing rooms, and the staff accommodations to the crafts food table lavishly laid out. Our first episode was the pilot, directed by Jim Burrows, the top director of pilots, and was greeted with very favorable reviews. Tony played a detective for the New Jersey State Police, stationed in the Hudson Street Precinct house. His character also had an ex-wife and a young son and was balancing all of this with an affair with the local crime reporter, played by Lori Loughlin. I was playing the lieutenant in charge of Hudson Street.

Lee Shallat Chemel took over, directing the show from then on.

Everything went along smoothly and was great fun, Tony being a positive element every day. Soon, however, it appeared there was controversy brewing as to the 8:30 p.m. time slot; It was rumored that Tony felt the early slot wasn't adult enough for the show and the network hierarchy didn't agree. Tony made it clear that he wanted a later time, somewhere in the nine to nine-thirty evening hour. I was never a party to the argument, but the word spread quickly that we were fighting with ABC which always meant the show was in trouble. But it was obvious that Tony was right as the ratings began to slip, our audience was too adult to tune in at such an early hour. The argument between ABC and Tony settled into a fight no one could win and soon we were frozen out to the point where the "suits" stopped covering our dress rehearsals. We did twenty-two half-hour episodes which aired from September 1995 to June 1996 and our second season was canceled. When I say canceled, I should say buried. There is no evidence of any repeats of Hudson Street, nor has it ever been mentioned in any news of renewals. ABC put the show and Tony Danza in a dark dungeon never to reappear. Lesson: never fight the suits.

Rob Schiller was establishing himself as a director, having worked with me as stage manager on *Santa Barbara*. He had written a short piece he wanted to film as part of his resume called *A Delicatessen Story*, starring Brad Garrett who had just landed a fine part on *Everyone Loves Raymond*. I did Rob the favor and schmoozed with Brad about my failed audition on *Raymond*. The film was sparse but very well directed and since I had some free time looming, I grabbed some tickets to the Olympics that were going on in Atlanta, Georgia at the time and flew to New York.

Joan and I were enjoying our favorite events at the Olympics, equestrian and aquatics, when a bomb went off not far from us, killing a woman just passing by the explosion. Everything was in chaos, but the events kept going on. A couple of days later I got a message on my phone to call the office. *Law & Order* was in a bind; they had to replace a major role, and could I get there quickly? We hated to leave the games, but the offer was too good to turn down. The script was waiting for me when we got back to New York. It was a terrific role and I started memorizing it that Tuesday night. I checked in Wednesday morning at the show's permanent studio in the Chelsea Piers buildings by the Hudson River. They were a one camera production, so I had three days of filming what was a truly important character in the episode they were doing. I was a judge in an interesting story of two women involved in a murder. My first scene was at the apartment where I was inspecting the evidence with my old friend Jerry Orbach, who was playing the main detective on the case. Additionally, my character was accused of sexual harassment by one of the assistant district attorneys, played by Carey Lowell. There was a dramatic scene of tensions between me and Sam Waterston who was eventually jailed by me after quite a long argument. To settle all these problems, I then have a scene with the DA, played by the fabulous actor, Steven Hill. I'm eventually discredited and lose my judgeship. This episode, dealing with sexual harassment in the workplace, was probably one of the first to address the problem as a main topic. To the show's credit, as it took several more years before so many horrific instances of sexual harassment and abuse within the industry came to light and were properly addressed. Of course, there's still a significant amount of work that needs to be done to ensure no one else suffers such injustice; perhaps focusing on establishing gender parity within the industry wherein more women and other marginalized people are given positions of power, there will be a marked decrease in toxic work environments that enable predatory behavior.

We had missed the finale of the Olympics so we enjoyed the arts of the city by taking in some theater and the Philharmonic, things only New York can offer. But the pleasures of theatergoing can last only for so long. It was back to work, as Richard Schmenner, the head of the New York Paradigm Group, was working on a film by Adam Bernstein called *Six Ways to Sunday*, a low-budget crime production about a young man who becomes associated with the local Mafia. The character offered to me was named Louis Varga, the Mafia boss, and I had a fine time ordering everyone around, whipping out my gun now and again, and being a loud mouth in general. Isaac Hayes, Debbie Harry, and Adrien Brody were in the cast. Adrien, of course, went on to win an Oscar a few years later. I had to hurry my scenes because *Mad About You* was calling.

It was great getting back to *Mad About You*. Paul and Helen greeted me like a lost brother, found at last. I got to do two episodes in a row before auditioning began. A promising one just before another *Mad About You* called me back. It was a Carol Leifer comedy called *Alright Already*. Ms. Leifer was a very successful writer on a number of ongoing hits like *The Larry Sanders Show*, *Seinfeld*, and *Saturday Night Live*. I auditioned to play her father, quickly got the part, and was set to do the pilot. She had gathered a group of actors who knew how to do comedy: Amy Yasbeck, Maury Sterling, Norm Crosby, Mitsi McCall, and directed brilliantly by my old partner, Rob Schiller. It was produced by Brad Grey and Bernie Brillstein on the WB Channel.

We were scheduled to do twenty-one half hour episodes and that regimen took nine months from September 1996 to May 1997. We had a lot of fun mostly, but that routine proved exhausting: the constant memorization, working on your feet all day, the stress of playing before a live audience, and doing it all with very little time off. It was nearly June when we finished and awaited the verdict if we were good enough to earn a second season. There were no prima donnas, very little back-biting and happily, Carol and I hit it off beautifully.

James Gandolfini and me in a 2 scene from The Sopranos. *Photo courtesy of HBO*

Mobsters all . . . Photo courtesy of HBO

The Sopranos *famous pork store shot in the first season. Photo courtesy of HBO*

12 David Chase. James Gandolfini. Vincent Pastore. Michael Imperioli. Steven Van Zandt. Richard Plepler.

I decided to spend the summer in New York waiting for a pick-up word. Joan was in the Asia on business, and I was fiddling around in a vacation house we bought in Connecticut. I was enjoying the time off, but it was becoming clear the show wasn't going to get picked up. Suddenly, I was stricken with terrible stomach pains and went back to my doctor in New York's Mount Sinai Hospital. I wound up with gastric problems and required an operation. The recuperation was pleasant, Joan flew back, and I lay there, bandaged heavily, just as David Chase called. Alisa had given David my number but didn't tell him where I was. He was quite friendly, we chatted about our days on *Northern Exposure*. Frankly I had no memory of seeing David Chase there, though I knew he had written some of the episodes I had filmed. Finally, he got around to why he was calling. He was doing a pilot named *The Sopranos,* and there was a cameo he wanted me to do. I assumed it was a rabbi or a

Jewish character because that kind of character was the basis of our relationship. I had no desire to do another Jewish person for fear of being typecast, but at my age that's ridiculous. His insistence was very effective, and it was an offer. I agreed. David said he would call the office and make a deal.

Before he hung up, he said, "see you Saturday."

I was bandaged in a hospital bed, but I wouldn't tell him that, I just said, "I do have a problem you should know about."

"What's that?" he asked.

"I don't sing."

He explained it wasn't a musical show, and that it was about a family in the New Jersey Mafia. The muscle of the group was Tony Soprano, hence the name. I had no idea how you leave a hospital in such a hurry. My surgeon, Daniel Popowich, advised against it, but I was out of there no matter what. I promised him I would be back the same day. He finally gave in and fixed me up with fresh bandages. That Friday night I strolled out like I was a visitor, in my street clothes. I spent the night in Joan's apartment where the show's van would pick me up; I didn't want anyone to know I was still a hospital patient. They did pick me up at the address I had given the staff. We went to a large parking area that had been roped off, mainly to keep gawkers away, though I didn't see any. After a quick greeting with David Chase, I relaxed in my dressing room van, learning the dialogue. All I had were the pages for the day. I had no idea what the subject was but after reading it through (two pages, mostly descriptive) I got the drift: I was threatening someone about the money this man owed Tony Soprano. Remarkably, the costumes laid out in the van were loose; a gymnasium-type sweatsuit and sneakers. It was exactly the kind of outfit that would hide the bandages around my stomach. Later when I questioned David about the casual attire, he explained that he saw Herman as a lawyer who spends a great deal of time lounging around. With that exchange I learned my character's name and profession. In my parlance, the scene was a quickie. Me and a character named Big Pussy, played by Vince Pastore, a well-known acting teacher and an old friend of mine from my Broadway days, had this scene on a bridge over a deep threatening gorge, with the obviously frightened guy. We did the scene a number of times, at different angles, and at no time was it ever discussed the rather large paunch Herman had.

There was a second piece to do. David said the scene was scheduled for Thursday of next week, a perfect four days away. I went back to the hospital: I told the teamster driver I was visiting a friend. The recuperation went well, and I was released on Monday, giving me plenty of time to work that week. The script was waiting for me at Joan's apartment, and it was a beaut. This was no cops and robbers junket, it was an odd mix of good and evil, life and death, and a fresh view inside the daily life of criminals and their easy violence. On top of that, David Chase brilliantly adds a female psychiatrist to whom Tony can unload in spite of the danger that someone will learn of this weakness. It was a great dramatic twist that could make this no ordinary crime show.

I was driven on Thursday to a raunchy strip club in New Jersey that they had named Bada Bing! I had learned the scene, read the script, and now knew what I was talking about. The scene was set in a small room overlooking the dance floor below with a few customers hanging around ogling the naked women, who were nonchalantly hanging onto their poles. The rest of the cast was already there, and we greeted each other then waited for David. They had been filming almost two weeks, so they knew each other and proceeded to fit me in. Michael Imperioli was younger than I thought when I read the script and James Gandolfini was a surprise. He wasn't an obscure actor, nor was he known. He was stocky, almost bald, and nowhere near what you would call a leading-man type. What he did have were the most searching, intelligent eyes I ever saw. Not handsome, but hugely charismatic. Earlier, when I read the full script, I learned why David was so hell bent to have me play Herman. Herman was an old friend of Tony's father who was in business with Herman, a Jew, which was frowned on in those days. In the scene he reports that Mahaffey has no money and has no wiggle-room to get it. Herman suggests a resolution which Tony elaborates on.

Tony then happily congratulates Herman, "You old fucking Jew. No wonder my old man kept you around so long."

It shows how much Tony leans on Herman as he messes with Herman's hair. The scene was pleasant to perform. I had a good take on everyone and the performances were first rate. Everything went beautifully. Handshakes all around, and well-wishes for the future. I paid my gratitude to David for thinking of me. When I got down to the main floor, one of the naked dancers shook my hand and told me that *Manhattan Murder Mystery* was her favorite movie.

The moment I agreed to do *Aftershock: Earthquake in New York*, I regretted it. It sounded interesting, and had a fine cast starring Tom Skerritt, Charles Dutton, Michael Moriarty, Cicely Tyson, and a cast of twenty-nine others. I was one of the others but that didn't bother me. What bothered me was what I read in a note from the director: *Are you afraid of heights? Can you swim? Does excess noise bother you? Are you strong enough to hold a person up?* It went on and on. I realized then that the special effects were going to be me.

I flew to Vancouver, Washington, checked into the hotel where we were to stay, and quickly met the director. His name was Mikael Salomon, a lovely Danish gentleman, who was known for being the Academy Award nominated cinematographer of James Cameron's *The Abyss*. The set was amazing; it was in an abandoned parking garage, not the whole place, just a sealed-off section that had been filled with water to make it look like a building or buildings that had collapsed into a maze. I was selected to be a sort of captain of a group of local hires, all members of an acting class based in Vancouver. They were all eager and delighted to have made it to the movies, so naturally they were ready to dive into the water-filled disaster scene no matter who gave the order. There is always a grumpy, negative loser at the party and, at this one, it was me. I was contracted for five days, all of which were spent in miserable, uncomfortable wetness. It didn't take a genius to know what Mikael Salomon had in store for the captain and his crew.

The first day was spent showing the area in which we would work, and we waded in the water just ankle deep. The water was warmed but it felt weird walking around in shoes and socks. After a while we all got used to it, though the water certainly looked dingy. The second day, inevitably, we were directed to use the entire area, waist deep this time. The feeling of being fully clothed, soaking wet, and trying to walk is extraordinarily tiring. I was given a flashlight and wandered through the water looking for a way out. The cameraman was in the water with us and shot us from different angles. Between shots, we sat in a green room of sorts, which was warmed and made the day bearable.

The third day was a surprise: no water. The scene was set back in time when all of us were covered in ashes and dust, which was somehow an improvement. We were searching for a way out as the building collapsed. It was made safe as the columns fell (they looked heavy but were lightweight) and we were done after two takes. My part was done, Mikael shook my hand as the crew applauded, and I went home after three horrid days in Vancouver. The only good thing that happened was that I got paid for five days but only worked three.

It was great to be back in California. The big news that greeted me was that Home Box Office had picked up their option on *The Sopranos* and would be going into production in March 1998, only a couple of months away. It reinforced my opinion about the show; it was unique material written brilliantly and capable of being a smash hit. The cast was a bunch of endearingly loony yet dangerous whackos the general public had never seen on television. Add David Chase to the mix and HBO has a boffo hit on their hands. Before I had a chance to call Alisa, she called me.

Richard Plepler, the head of programming at HBO, liked the character, "Hesh" so much that he discussed keeping him on the show with David Chase. David agreed with Plepler that a Jewish, semi-mobster on the fringes of the Italian clan could be quite useful dramatically. I already had a deal in place from the pilot that I had done the previous year, so if I agreed I would be a recurring cast member of *The Sopranos*, certainly a juicy spot. My only caveat, and a most important one that needed explanation, was if I'd be allowed other gainful employment during production, or if I'd be prevented from working elsewhere even when episodes I didn't appear in were being filmed? It took some time, but eventually it was agreed that I could do other things as long as *The Sopranos* had priority.

The show was being produced in New York City which gave Joan and me some unbroken, quality time together. Headquarters were in the old Silvercup bread building just over the 59th Street Bridge in Long Island City. All it took was two stops on the 4 train and you were there. Before my first day of filming, I had a great meeting with David at his hotel. He explained Hesh's backstory as he had created it; Hesh and Tony's father, Johnny, had a business together in the Jukebox racket and he became Tony's mentor even though Hesh was never a *made man* because he was Jewish. Everybody treated Hesh with respect mainly because Tony relied on him. The meeting gave me an excellent tool in playing the role during the entire run of the show.

SPOILER ALERT

Dear Reader: if you still have not seen *The Sopranos*, or at least know how it ends, (even after decades since its release), then skip ahead to Chapter 16. Then come back and read what you missed!

On my first day back in March 1998, I was driven to a hospital in New Jersey where we were to shoot a scene with Jackie Aprile, played by Michael Rispoli, the present boss who was dying of cancer. It gave me a chance to meet and renew my relationship with James Gandolfini, who greeted me with a tremendous bear hug. He introduced me all around to people I was going to interact with for years. I knew Vincent Pastore and Michael Imperioli, who was to have a major role in the series as Tony's nephew. I learned, during conversations off camera, that Rispoli was the runner up to play Tony Soprano, and here he was about to die off on the show. It made for an odd day.

After a day off, I was back at the hospital for episode three, which seemed to me to be one of the reasons I was on the show. Big Pussy (Vince Pastore) and Paulie Walnuts (Tony Sirico) were having trouble with an Hasidic owner of a motel who wouldn't pay protection, and during another hospital scene with Jackie, they ask me how to handle this guy. I explain the code of honor and the strength of character "these people" possess and the stubbornness the guys are up against. By the way, Hesh is greeted by Aprile very respectfully as one of the guys. Before our scene was called, I watched a hilarious scene being shot, with Tony, Aprile, and a nurse. I was wondering who the actress was while I sat in the make-up van next to her. I watched the action from video village, the name that the production area is called. The nurse enters and fixes Jackie's covers then proceeds to undress and give him Tony's get well *present*. Entirely naked she climbs into his bed as Tony enters laughing hysterically. She was amazing standing around like that while they did the scene a few times.

There was some free time now before episode four was scheduled. I had heard of a play by Elaine May that was being directed by Alan Arkin and was auditioning people. The play was called *Taller Than a Dwarf* and was to star Matthew Broderick. Beyond the lousy title, the production had a terrific pedigree, so I decided to audition. My loony idea was that if I got the play, I could do *The Sopranos* during the day and *Taller Than a Dwarf* at night, a totally ridiculous scenario. Well, I auditioned, Alan Arkin hugged me, and I thought they were going to offer me the part of Matthew Broderick's father.

The day we shot episode four had to be the hottest day in history. It was a scene with the full cast at Jackie Aprile's funeral. There was a lot going on and many takes, as the scene involves the FBI taking pictures of the gang surreptitiously. All I had to do was stand there, next to Tony, looking professional, and stand there, and stand there. I thought at any minute they would have to carry me out of there or bury me there along with Jackie Aprile. It really was a tough day, worse than *Earthquake* in Vancouver, but I was a trouper and made it.

I had to wait a few weeks to do my first scene with James Gandolfini. It was a 2 *scene,* a scene with only two actors, in episode six where I threaten to cut my association with the mob, due to the exorbitant taxation Uncle Junior has made in Hesh's cut. It was a well written scene that showed the affection both men felt for each other, and it was a pleasure to work with Jim alone. We did the scene a number of times, and at the finish, Jim put his arm on my shoulder and said: "Wow, that was great!" There was an additional scene in the episode with Dominic Chianese and the gang in which Tony bargains a truce between Hesh and Uncle Junior. A very agreeable episode, but not my favorite, which was coming next.

It took almost a month of waiting to do episode ten, but it was worth the wait. It had to do with reparations and a character named Massive Genius, played by a fine actor, Bokeem Woodbine. In the episode, Massive Genius claimed Hesh personally owed his family for work done decades ago. Since Hesh was now a successful Jew, Massive Genius insinuated that he must have skimmed money that was owed to the black artists who recorded for Hesh's F-Note Records. The writing was enjoyably witty and dramatic, as accusations were flung by both Hesh and Massive Genius ending with a powerful retort from Hesh: "You're talking to the wrong white man, my friend. My people were the white man's n****r when yours were still painting their faces and chasing zebras." These scenes were the first time *The Sopranos* dealt with the similarities and conflicts between Italian, Jewish, and African American communities, organized crime, and popular culture.

In another scene, Michael Imperioli's character, Christopher, wants Hesh's opinion on a song he's produced. Obviously, Hesh hates the record and says: "I know when a hit is a hit. And that is no hit, my friend." The episode was filled with great characters, great scenes, and memorable dialogue. A *hit* is a *hit*.

Meryl Streep, Uma Thurman, and me in Prime. *Photo courtesy of Universal Studios Licensing LLC*

13

**Elaine May. Alan Arkin.
Matthew Broderick. Parker Posey.
Joanne Whalley. Nancy Marchand.
Aida Turturro. Bob Saget.
Brie Larson. Kat Dennings.**

There was a long hiatus now, and with permission from the show, I accepted the offer to appear in the play, *Taller Than a Dwarf*. Both parties agreed to my schedule with the play; my appearances in episodes of *The Sopranos* would be during the day, ending in time to get to the theater, and I would be excused from taping on Wednesdays. It required cooperation from both sides, which I greatly appreciated, and I think everyone knew I wanted to be onstage in a Broadway production after spending some thirty years backstage.

However, when I got the script to the play, I was mortified! As bad as the title was, the play was worse! Talk about boring, unfunny, and the epitome of wishful thinking, this was *it*. With all the great talent involved in this project, I expected all its shortcomings would be improved. Casting was in place and, in addition to Matthew Broderick, there was Parker Posey playing the role of his character's wife, Joyce Van Patten playing the role of my character's wife, and

Marcia Jean Kurtz. Rehearsals began in March 1999 right after I finished episode ten on *The Sopranos*.

We worked on the play, which was about a couple of New Yorkers experiencing mid-life crisis, for a little more than three weeks without changing much in terms of structure or dialogue. We were scheduled to do two weeks of previews in Boston where I anticipated major improvements would be made, away from the prying eyes of Broadway pundits. I was still unscheduled for the next episode of *The Sopranos*, and I felt the trip would work wonders on the play. Here it comes, wishful thinking and what Phil Adler once brilliantly said: "Whatever problems you have when you get on the train in New York, that's what gets off in Boston." And there were plenty. The major problem was making the piece into a solid play with the usual overused requirement: a beginning, a middle, and an end. Not having any of that, what we did have was a sitcom ready for television. The Boston reviews made it clear; we had an enormous amount of work to do to make it into a play.

After two weeks in Boston, I don't think we changed a comma or a meaningful situation. It was aggravating to see the combined talents of Elaine May and Alan Arkin end in stalemate. Advice from Stanley Donen, Ms. May's engaged partner overseeing the production, didn't seem to help either. In cases like this, there's always a stream of suggestions coming from the actors involved, who know the ways to make the thing a hit, but nobody listens. The Boston run of the play unfortunately ended with much tension. To repeat the Adler-ism I noted previously, "Whatever you put on the train in Boston, that's what gets off in New York." Unfortunately, I now knew *The Sopranos* had become the rage of television, making Sunday night a must with the majority of TV viewers glued to their sets. Vincent Canby, in the *New York Times*, wrote that "'Berlin Alexanderplatz,' 'The Singing Detective' and 'The Sopranos' are something more than mini-series . . . they are not open-ended series, or even mini-series. They are megamovies."[14] On the other hand, *Taller Than a Dwarf* was greeted at the other end of the spectrum, being called rather "an elongated sketch than a real play."[15]

Obviously, I had made a terrible mistake performing this dull play night after night and twice on Wednesday and Saturday while the entire second season of *The Sopranos* was being produced. David Chase was being kind to me, keeping me in the flow of the show's episodes. During the run of *Taller Than a Dwarf*, five months at the Longacre Theater, I did four episodes of *The Sopranos* and only one was of any importance except to establish that Johnny, Tony's father, also suffered from fainting spells. I appeared mainly as background at parties and at the hospital when Christopher had been shot. Amazingly, I was a big hit coming out of the Longacre stage door with Hesh fans asking for my autograph.

Taller Than a Dwarf opened in March 2000 and closed in June of that year during which I snuck in my *Sopranos* episodes. Waiting for the third season to begin, I was lucky enough to get cast in a TV Movie called *Jackie Bouvier Kennedy Onassis,* which had Joanne Whalley playing Jackie. I had adored Ms. Whalley ever since she played a nurse that could make you happy to be hospitalized: she was memorable in my favorite television play, Dennis Potter's *The Singing Detective,* produced by the BBC in London years ago. This production starred Tom Skerrit, Tim Matheson, Diane Baker, Frances Fisher, and Philip Baker Hall as Onassis. I was cast as Maurice Templesman, her last love. It was a terrific gig, driving round New York City in August, doing scenes in an air-conditioned

---

14 Canby, Vincent. 1999. "From the Humble Mini-Series Comes the Magnificent Megamovie." *The New York Times,* October 31, 1999. https://www.nytimes.com/1999/10/31/arts/from-the-humble-mini-series-comes-the-magnificent-megamovie.html.
15 Taylor, Markland. 2000. "Taller Than a Dwarf." *Variety,* March 13, 2000. https://variety.com/2000/legit/reviews/taller-than-a-dwarf-1200461160/.

limo with the brilliant Ms. Whalley. The show got quite favorable reviews, and, curiously, I got to play Maurice in love with Jackie while Joanne played Jackie, a person she adored.

I got back in time for the third season of *The Sopranos* but there was very little for the character of Hesh to do. Having been away from the show doing a television movie and a Broadway play, I think the writers had lost confidence in my being available for storylines like the regulars. As a result, I was included in scenes but rarely as a main character. The first episode of the new season was a big party at the Soprano's home, which was a kind of a reintroduction of everyone since the show had been away for many months. My next scene was a dinner where the Patsy character, who was harboring a hatred of Tony because Tony had been involved in Patsy's twin brother's death. That was the main drama of the scene, which was being played out while the gang was having a sit-down lunch of spaghetti and meatballs. Because of retakes, single shots, and close-ups of the many faces at the table, we wound up eating spaghetti and meatballs for six hours. Try and eat spaghetti and meatballs for six hours and it manages to become a terrible task and an unforgivable torture. We had to make the most of it by relieving ourselves after each take in little buckets we each had by our sides.

Shocking news came of the death of our beloved Nancy Marchand, who played Tony's mother, Livia, on the show. Nancy had been suffering from an incurable cancer from the first days of the show, but she carried that burden uncomplainingly in every scene she did. She was amazing. When a major cast member dies or leaves the production, it inevitably alters the future plans of the show. In this case, the writers had made storylines ready in light of Ms. Marchand's illness, as it was known from the beginning. In the show, Janice, Livia's daughter, creates a memorial much to Tony's opposition and displeasure, allowing for an extraordinary dramedy scene; everyone stands around not knowing how to break the ice until Janice nails Hesh to open the proceedings. She acknowledges Hesh has known Livia the longest and must have something to say about her. Hesh, caught speechless, fumbles and describing Livia says, "Between brain and mouth, was no interlocutor." That was a classic moment I had in that episode, but there proved to be not much more for Hesh in the rest of the season. I checked quietly with Robin Green and Mitchell Burgess, who were writers on staff and friends from our *Northern Exposure* days, if they felt the Hesh character was truly secondary in David Chase's mind. They thought Hesh would become more important as the show slowed down. As of then, I felt that I had become less reliable because I had other things to do rather than wait for work at *The Sopranos* office.

Soon after, I got an offer to do a series with Bob Saget, a favorite on television. The show was called *Raising Dad*, and I was to be Bob's father. The appetizing aspect of the offer was simple: The WB Network guaranteed twenty-two episodes coupled with a ludicrous amount of money for me. *The Sopranos* was going to lay off for a long time, almost a year as it turned out, so how could a sane person ignore the deal. Besides Bob and me, the family was comprised of Kat Dennings as the older sister and Brie Larson as the younger sister. Bob Saget turned out to be one of the wittiest, funniest performers I ever knew, and his work ethic made coming to work every day a pleasure. We did the usual three weeks with the fourth week off which gave me time to get home once a month. The show was quite funny and topical, loaded with young people giving Bob lots of trouble at home, and even more trouble in his role as a high school teacher. I had an especially lovely time playing scenes with Brie, answering a million questions she asked about show business. I had a feeling Brie would have a successful career, and she certainly exceeded all expectations by winning the Academy Award for Best Actress for her breathtaking performance in *Room*. Kat was also excellent on the show and, of course, went on to the hugely popular sitcom, *2 Broke Girls,* as well as a successful film career. We did the show from October 2001 until May 2002 and enjoyed every moment of it. In the end, and for some questionable reason, the suits canceled us, never taking advantage of the extraordinary talents of Bob Saget.

In Her Shoes *with Shirley MacLaine & Cameron Diaz*

Meryl Streep. Richard Schiff.
Uma Thurman. Shirley MacLaine.
Cameron Diaz. Polly Bergen.

I got called back to *The Sopranos* in the fall of 2002 to do some episodes for season four. The episodes established Hesh's racehorses, particularly Pie-O-My, a horse Tony loved and came to own. Tony seemed to have a greater affinity for the horse than for most people.

Another break in time proved very fruitful. It was early winter, and I got a fabulous break. I got a call to do the Christmas episode of *The West Wing*, one of my favorite television shows and certainly among the most honored. My episode was called "Holy Night," and it concerned Toby Ziegler, who was played by the greatly talented Richard Schiff. There had been a long-standing rift between Toby and his father, Jules Ziegler, whom I had the pleasure of playing, a former member of the Brooklyn gang, Murder, Incorporated, but now on parole. Jules Ziegler had come to the White House to try and make amends and have Toby join him in a visit with the Ziegler family. Naturally Toby was aghast at having an ex-convict wandering around the West Wing being "a threat to the President," which Jules pledges he is not. The scenes with Mr. Schiff were deeply emotional and interesting mainly because he is a wonderful actor, and the dialogue was written by Aaron Sorkin. It was eerie leaving my apartment in Burbank and being on *The West Wing* set four blocks away; the place is so authentic you think you'll bump into the real people at any turn. I hated leaving the show after one episode, so I suggested they should make Jules the Attorney General since he had so much experience with the law. Not surprisingly, my suggestion garnered no response.

A feature film, my first since *Manhattan Murder Mystery*, came my way. The movie was *Prime*, starring Meryl Streep, Uma Thurman, Tony Collette, and Bryan Greenberg—not a bad lot. I had an informal audition with the director, Ben Younger, who I joked was "a hell of a lot younger than me." We seemed to enjoy each other's company and I got the part. I was cast as Meryl Streep's father, an opportunity I relished. It was terrific schmoozing with Meryl who had a house in Salisbury, Connecticut near mine. In the plot of the movie, Meryl was Lisa Bloomberg, a therapist with an office on the Upper West Side of New York, and Uma was a patient of hers. Uma, a woman in her mid-thirties, was having an affair with a much younger (there goes that word again) man in his twenties. Sandra Bullock was originally cast in the role but pulled out over creative differences and Ms. Thurman replaced her.

The twist in the movie came when Meryl realizes Uma is talking (and very intimately) about Meryl's son, David. There are a lot of funny situations in the film, one of the most memorable being when David decides to bring Uma to meet the family at a Friday night dinner. In that scene, where I meet Uma for the first time, I spontaneously uttered "wow," as she walked in. Ben, the director, loved it and we kept it in the film. Meryl, taking on all the characteristics of an Upper West Side momma, brought cookies and little candies to the green room every day. When she heard my wife, Joan, and me discussing Joan's imminent birthday, she came in the next day carrying a huge birthday cake. She was truly a friend in no time, it was amazing. I watched her, remembering that astonishing performance in *Sophie's Choice*, arguably the finest in movie history, and how she had mastered accents and mannerisms in her amazing body of work.

It's a little egotistical to say, "I'm doing a movie with Meryl Streep and Uma Thurman," when, in reality, you're just having dinner with them in the picture and it's a "don't blink, or you'll miss me" sort of thing. The damn dinner took two days and reminded me of eating meat balls with Jimmy Gandolfini. I bet I carved that brisket twenty times. In the end, it was a lot of fun. The sad part comes as you finish your role and do all the goodbyes, just like in the theater when the curtain falls for the last performance; all those treasured friendships, made under tension and pressure, simply fade away never to be revived. But I collaborated with Meryl Streep, and even if it was for a brief time, it was an experience to be remembered.

Paradigm called and jokingly asked me if I would mind playing Shirley MacLaine's paramour (I would like to be anything Shirley wants) in a new movie called *In Her Shoes* to be directed by Curtis Hanson. I had literally just finished my work on *Prime*, so good news was coming in bushel baskets. In addition to Ms. MacLaine, the cast included Cameron Diaz, Toni Collette, Francine Beers, and Ken Howard. Mr. Hanson was directing a script by Jennifer Weiner. The movie revolved around two sisters, one a conservative lawyer, Ms. Collette, and the other a free spirit, Ms. Diaz, whose life and work are affected by a severe case of dyslexia. Through mishaps and misunderstandings, the feud between the sisters boils over, and Cameron's character finds herself visiting her grandmother, Ms. MacLaine, in Florida at a senior community. The movie was shot in Delray Beach, and I had a nice apartment with an ocean view. On days off, I lazed by the pool along with the lovely and talented Cameron Diaz. Back on the set, it was machinations galore, and the sisters were reunited along with their grandmother. One of the scenes takes place at a dance at the senior living center wherein Shirley and I were staged to dance, at which time my character, madly in love with Shirley's character, grabs a kiss while we're doing the foxtrot. In rehearsals, Shirley whispered in my ear concerning the kiss, "no tongue! I mean it. No tongue, or I'll bite it!" Of course, I was a true gentleman and gave her a nice, juicy pucker job.

When I was back in New York and quite pleased with myself, having done *The West Wing*, two feature films, and played scenes with the likes of Meryl Streep, Shirley MacLaine, Cameron Diaz, and Richard Schiff, Paradigm's New York office welcomed me back in town and told me *The Sopranos* wanted to know if I would be free to do season five, starting quite soon. It was now the middle of 2004, and production began in earnest. The season emphasized Adriana's problems with the FBI, her confession to Christopher that she had indeed worn a wire, and her subsequent execution in a harrowing scene with Silvio. The B story concerned Hesh. At Aunt Concetta's funeral, Tony meets Fanny, played by Polly Bergen. Fanny had been Johnny Boy's longtime mistress and Tony spends some interesting time with Fanny learning more about his father's youth. In sympathy with her modest situation, Tony wants Hesh and Leotardo to cut her in on their racetrack's profits, like Johnny Boy had intended. Hesh resists sharing money with "some old hag" but finally agrees to help Fanny. It was a fascinating story played remarkably by Ms. Bergen. During all of this, rumors were afloat that "every show, even the good ones, close."

The great fire Lt. Feinberg on Rescue Me

Richard Schiff & me on The West Wing. *Photo by Warner Bros. Television*

15 | Sidney Lumet. David Caruso. Larry David. Philip Seymour Hoffman. Charlie Kaufman. Denis Leary. Christine Baranski. Julianna Margulies.

The show went on a long hiatus, again, and now being a New York actor, I hunkered down and enjoyed the city. I hadn't hunkered long, when I got a call from the office to meet the great screen director, Sidney Lumet. He directed *12 Angry Men*, *Network*, and a favorite of mine, *Dog Day Afternoon*. We met in Mr. Lumet's office, and he was so impressed by my work, I almost lost it. He wanted me in the picture, by all means, but there was a problem: he wanted me to play the role of the judge, but he had already offered the role to Ron Silver, a veteran Broadway actor. He said if Ron turned the part down, I would be the judge. He gave me the script and we shook hands. Unbelievable, an offer from Sidney Lumet!

I read the script as soon as I got home, and I wasn't so excited. The movie was about the longest Mafia trial in history. There was Vin Diesel in the lead and nineteen other mobsters. Vin's character was acting as his own lawyer and the judge sat there in every scene, not saying much. It would be heroic not to fall asleep during those endless trial scenes. I could never be so rude as to turn down a Lumet offer so I lit candles and prayed Ron Silver would take the part. God was on my side and Ron Silver accepted the part. Lumet was the only disappointed person in this triangle, and he insisted I play Rizzo, Diesel's lawyer, who he fires before the trial begins. Perfect.

I had two scenes; the first was at lunch with Vin at an outdoor restaurant on City Island. In the scene, Vin is pleading with me to be more active in his defense and I'm more interested in lunch. I was absolutely knocked off my knickers at Sidney Lumet's total preparation and direction. I was on the set by 9:30 a.m., took a seat at the table, greeted Mr. Diesel, and ran the scene for the cameras. Sidney asked me to pay little attention to Vin and more on the food. We shot the scene four times before he said "*Cut!*" and I was on my way home before noon. Holy moly, that was amazing. Four days later, we shot the second of my scenes, where I meet with Vin in a prison cell in Trenton, New Jersey. The scene was short. Vin's character was upset at the way I was handling his case, we argued, and he fired me, taking on his own defense at trial. It took an hour and a half, and I was done with the movie and shaking hands with Vin Diesel and Sidney Lumet. What an experience, not only to meet this great man, but to work with him—very quickly.

Think of the most ridiculous piece of casting you can conceive of and, I guarantee, this one is more ludicrous: Jerry Adler as Cardinal Bennedetti of the Roman Catholic Church! Crazy, huh? Well somewhere down the line, someone thought it was a great fit and there I was flying down to Miami to do *CSI: Miami.* I kid you not. They put me up overnight and picked me up in the morning. They had their own studio, and I was ushered into the costume department where we all had enough guffaws to last an eternity. After all the fittings were done, I had the costumer get a shot of me on my iPhone—a picture I shall treasure forever. An assistant director took me to the set, which was a confessional booth erected in limbo. No one laughed or even giggled as I came on set, so maybe the only ones who thought this was hilarious were me, the costumer, and the world. I was introduced to the director, Mr. Rob Zombie. The whole thing was taking on some surrealistic weirdness, but I tried my best to be a professional. Mr. Zombie escorted me to my seat in the booth and he ran the cameras for focus. The penitent was to be played by their star, David Caruso, and Mr. Caruso's stand-in and I ran the scene for the crew. I mean it was totally whacko to have me flown down there to do this scene, as I had three words to say and Caruso had seven, but I was determined to be a good boy.

There was a kind of hush when they brought Mr. Caruso onto the stage, and I remembered the rumors that he was *trouble* everywhere he went. We were introduced, and I stuck my bejeweled hand out—he just nodded. As we got into the booth, I saw the stand-in running for the hills, so I steeled myself as we settled in. He didn't like the stool on his side. There was much discussion about what kind of seat would work and the prop man went out to get a proper seat. Meanwhile, Caruso suggested we run the lines, which we did, a couple of times. That went quickly since there were only ten words to run. He questioned his dialogue, wondering if his words were accurate and Mr. Zombie assured him that the scene was letter perfect. The prop man came back with an assortment of chairs and stools, and we proceeded to rehearse on the set. As directed, when Mr. Zombie called "*Action!*" I slid open the little portal door which revealed the mesh between us, but he said, "I can't see him. Is he there? It's all red." That prompted more discussion. Was I sitting too high? Was he too low? Not one of the pieces of furniture the prop guy found was any good. They decided to lower my chair and build a little riser for him. While construction began, Mr. Caruso went back to his dressing room to rest. I grabbed one of the unused chairs and watched the action. When Mr. Zombie and the stand-in agreed they could see me, we sent for the star.

"He really likes you. He really does," Mr. Zombie happily whispered in my ear.

What the hell did I care what he thinks? All I wanted at that moment was to say my words and get crackin' out of there. It staggers me to come across guys like this who bring their troubles onstage with them, making more money in a day than the whole crew makes in a week and yet, there's no end to the coddling and fawning they demand. I guess we learn to live with it or move on. We did the first part, which was mainly MOS (Mit Out Sound, or without sound), a set-up of Caruso arriving and entering the confessional. Next, they moved in closer for the second part of the scene. We got ready, Mr. Zombie called *"Action!"* and I slid open the little door.

"Yes, my son," I said.

"Forgive me, Fa—"

Mr. Zombie yelled *"Cut!"* Then, he and Caruso went into discussions I couldn't quite make out. I think it concerned the stress he should put on the word "forgive," whether he should accentuate *FOR*give or use the accent on for*GIVE*. I was willing to forgive anything, so long as we got it done. I had already missed my flight home, so this crap could go on all night since I was entering overtime. It was decided to tape it both ways and after many complaints: he didn't like the screen, he couldn't hear me, I was too loud, the little door should open slowly for dramatic purpose or maybe it shouldn't, he began to run out of excuses and at the end of a long day, this ten-word scene came to an end. Nobody said anything to me, as Mr. Zombie and Caruso left the stage, congratulating each other. The first AD released me, and I made a beeline to my dressing room, changed, and fled.

It was officially announced that season six was to be the final season of *The Sopranos*, ending its tremendously successful run. The writers had spent many months scripting the finale and everyone involved was notified to be available. I got the call and informed the office of my availability. But before we met for the last table reading of the first episode, it was announced that there would be a season seven. It seems HBO had some contractual issues and decided to divide the show's final run into twelve episodes as season six and a final nine episodes called season seven. In the scheduling rehash, I wound up with episodes in both seasons.

The best way to prepare your audience that the production will be closing down is to kill the star of the show. That's what it seemed was about to happen as the dementia-stricken Uncle Junior shoots Tony and puts him into a deep coma where we wonder if he will ever recover. That was followed with episodes wherein Tony must fight for his identity and future, and the show began tying things up: Silvio can't handle responsibilities, Paulie has cancer, Ray Curto is murdered, Eugene Pontecorvo hangs himself, Meadow plans to divorce Finn, Artie's restaurant suffers extreme competition, Johnny Sack dies in prison after suffering a demeaning arrest at his daughter's wedding, Vito is heading for disaster, and so on as each character slowly exits the stage, their sins catching up to them. Hesh had very little to do except add to Tony's vigil, but I was sure my time would come in season seven.

There was to be another hiatus before season seven was scheduled to start, and Larry David put me into an episode of *Curb Your Enthusiasm*. I also met Denis Leary at a Young People's poem reading event in Roxbury, Connecticut where we both lived. Denis was a huge fan of *The Sopranos* and said he would love to have me join him in his FX series, *Rescue Me*. It was great having things in the hopper, waiting to go.

The *Curb Your Enthusiasm* episode was about Larry looking for an agreeable man to hold a minyan in his apartment; a minyan refers to the ten men over the age of thirteen needed to hold a Jewish religious event. In the scene I'm stopped by Larry in the street in front of his building and after much pleading and agonizing, I agree to join him and another gentleman he has with him in a quick meeting upstairs. We meet the waiting group of men in yarmulkes, anxious to get started with their meeting when it is discovered that the other man Larry brought in is Bill Buckner, the retired Boston Red Sox first baseman whose error gave the New York Mets the 1986 World Series Championship. All of this was happening in pure improv since no one had a script. Fierce controversy broke out as soon as Mr. Buckner was recognized; there were Red Sox and Mets fans, guys from New England, others from Brooklyn, all at each other's throats. But most of the hatred was directed at poor Bill Buckner—I, however, being a life-long Mets fan, insisted that he was my favorite baseball player of all time. The whole thing was a riot, even Bill enjoyed it.

I know it seems I leap from one project to the next but that is never the case. There are long, undefined periods in which you wonder if it's all over and the future is quickly evolving into a present where most men of my age sit back and survive on pensions. It was slowly beginning to feel that way during the very long lull *The Sopranos* took. I filled the time as I always did, auditioning and networking in an attempt to delay retirement. One of my auditions was really a meeting and an extraordinarily interesting one: Charlie Kaufman, a gifted screenwriter and novelist, famed for writing *Being John Malkovich* and winning an Oscar for writing *Eternal Sunshine of the Spotless Mind*. He had been associated with the director

Spike Jonze, but he was now directing his first feature about which we were meeting. *Synecdoche, New York* was a film about a director in crisis, having lost his family and career, who is planning a theatrical event no one else will touch. As we met and talked, I had the feeling *Synecdoche, New York* was mainly about Charlie Kaufman. The movie had a dynamite cast: Philip Seymour Hoffman, Jennifer Jason Leigh, Emma Watson, Catherine Keener, Diane Wiest, Michelle Williams, and Samantha Morton. It looked like he had cast nearly every fine actress in the business, plus Lynne Cohen as Hoffman's mother and possibly, if our meeting went well, me as his father. Well, the meeting was lovely and incredibly interesting with Kaufman ruminating about screenwriting, film directing, and life in general. I got the part and retirement would have to wait.

Reading the script, I was convinced it had no possibility of being a commercial success; it was one of those brilliant arthouse films that most people didn't understand but loved. How else could he have gathered such an incredible cast except that they met, were dazzled by him, and were eager to do this intricate, but fascinating film. I didn't have much to do in the movie, but it was so pleasant joining this group during breaks and discussing politics, and all the hot topics of the day. They seemed to gather like a beach party cookout every time we waited for another set-up, Hoffman included, smoking one cigarette after the other. He was as intelligent as Charlie and between them and the incredible actresses on set, I relished the off-camera time more than the job. Plus, the rented house in Brooklyn we filmed in was identical to my Aunt Dorothy and Uncle Nat's place where I visited many, many times in childhood. It was strange, yet nostalgic. I finished my part in the film in less than a week and sadly left after a very heartfelt exchange with Charlie. I always wondered why Charlie never called himself Charles, but then again, I never liked Jerome.

Season seven of *The Sopranos* started without me. Having read the script, I knew my participation in the outstanding and eagerly anticipated finish to television's most watched and discussed event in broadcast history. A program that made Home Box Office a premiere cable staple, made household names of many performers on the show, and placed David Chase at the top tier of screenwriters. Not to mention the enormous wealth he accrued and the bonanza he would make, and undoubtedly deserved when *The Sopranos* reached reruns. But Carmela was right when she said, "everything ends." Every show, the good ones and the bad; every play, television series, every story line you love and enjoy, finishes; the curtain falls inexorably. And, so it was with us, and it was no fun being around the place as the inevitable past catches up to everyone: Bobby gets shot dead, Leotardo to follow, and worst of all, we see the end of Christopher at the hands of his uncle, Tony Soprano.

My end was not sudden but was worse than a quick kill. Hesh had been covering Tony's debts while Tony was losing badly at roulette and the losses were staggering while Tony was on this crazy gambling binge he couldn't stop. Hesh was critical of Tony's outrageous spending including a purchase of a yacht for two-and-a-half million dollars. The rift began to fester the more Tony was out of touch with reality. During this problem between them, Renata, Hesh's girlfriend, suddenly and strangely, dies in their bedroom. It is never discussed, but Hesh slowly harbors a feeling that Tony or his gang on Tony's orders were responsible in some way for her death. I never got a direct answer when I questioned the writers, but they must have whacked her to punish Hesh's endless queries for money he rightly deserved.

The final scene, a sad, and amazing scene where Tony, totally unsympathetic of Hesh's grief, tosses a bag of money, clearing their debt, right next to Hesh, who is seated unkempt and alone. Tony says, "sorry for your loss," and leaves, ending what had been a very close and faithful relationship. It was as shocking as if Tony had pulled a gun. And that was my final scene on *The Sopranos*, a job I was associated with for ten years, on and off. Jimmy and I both knew we were not scheduled for another scene together and we hugged, exchanged great admiration for each other, and vowed to work on another show together sometime soon. It never happened. A tragic loss none of us will ever forget. Rest in peace, dear friend.

I was at home watching the show when its final episode aired. What a confusing and inexplicable moment when the screen cut to black. The credit roll explained everything. There could have been what most of us expected, some wild gangland shoot-out or the wise guy who went to the toilet and came out shooting or the diner door opening to reveal some mobsters blazing away and killing everyone. One of those options fit the general expectation. But I think David would have none of that. What he wanted was controversy, everybody talking about the ending, giving their opinions, keeping *The Sopranos* alive, forever. And so, it is still alive, an endless topic. One thing is for sure, David could never kill Tony Soprano.

It was strange not having *The Sopranos* to lean on for employment after so many years, but I started auditioning again and found myself enjoying the process, meeting casting directors, and fellow actors looking for work. I popped a job after a while; it was on Michael Imperioli's new crime drama called *Detroit 1-8-7*. Unbeknownst to anyone, my grandson, Joe Adler, had auditioned for the same show and was successful. Joe, in his early twenties, blonde, very talented, and handsome, had become a favorite young actor. Curiously, he wasn't cast as my nephew in the show because he didn't look enough like me, so he played one of my gang of young ruffians. We met as a surprise to him on the set in Detroit. It's amazing how anybody gets cast in anything.

Meanwhile, Jack McGee, who had been playing the fire chief on *Rescue Me* wanted to return to his home in California after three years on the show. Denis Leary, true to his wish to have me on the show when *The Sopranos* ended, quickly made a deal for me and so I became Fire Chief Sidney Feinberg. The show was an FX drama produced and written by Peter Tolan, whom I had done a pilot for, and Evan Reilly, a very successful writer and co-producer on the show. He was also the son of my old friend, Frank Reilly, a realtor working with my brother, Mike. It really is a small world.

I joined *Rescue Me* in its fourth year. It was 2009 and I was seventy-nine years old, a little too old for a fireman, but who's counting? The drama centered around Tommy Gavin played by Denis Leary, a troubled man divorced and involved with other lovers. He is also a heroic fireman, as all of them are in reality. The series had a very large cast, but I was involved only with the men in the firehouse. That group included Steve Pasquale, Daniel Sunjata, Michael Lombardi, John Scurti, and Larenz Tate. I found them to be a foul-mouthed, cigarette smoking, fun-loving gang enjoying themselves every moment of the day. The clouds of smoke were so thick I wondered how the cameras could find the stage. The production had commandeered an abandoned firehouse in Brooklyn's Red Hook District and had taken it over. They had renovated, refitted, and equipped the building so completely it seemed to be a working facility. There was a tenement building two blocks from the firehouse that was used to simulate actual fires, and a retired fireman was hired to oversee scenes where fire effects were used. It really was a professional set-up.

The last days of *Rescue Me* were hectic for everyone as we tied up all the loose ends. I even went to a fire event, all dolled up in my full regalia, including my Chief's helmet which weighed a ton and made me look like an idiot. The farewells were grim having spent years together and knowing our paths would certainly diverge; Denis had some great irons in the fire ahead, I knew Steve Pasquale was a hot item, Dan Sunjata already had a job in Hollywood waiting for him, and Michael Lombardi had a band and real bookings. I didn't worry about Pete Tolan or Evan Reilly, as good writers are in quick demand, and they were two of the best.

During the waning days of the run, I auditioned for a two-scene bit in *The Good Wife*, a very successful CBS drama then in its second year. On the show, there was a Board of Trustees meeting coming up and the group headed by Christine Baranski and Josh Charles needed one more vote to win the day. They wanted to get the lawyer who once owned the firm and still had voting rights: Enter Howard Lyman, a semi-retired lawyer, played by me. I did the scenes during my last summer break on *Rescue Me* and had a great time with Josh, a lifelong Broadway enthusiast.

Guess who in A Most Violent Year

Memorable scene with Michael J. Fox

16

Michelle & Robert King. Robin Williams. Peter Dinklage. Zachary Levi. Gael García Bernal. Oscar Isaac. Jessica Chastain. Al Pacino. Robert De Niro. Jason Alexander. Joey Soloway. Brian Dennehy. Paul Rudd. Abbi Jacobson. Ilana Glazer.

Speaking of being in demand, Michelle and Robert King, the creators of *The Good Wife*, felt the Howard Lyman character added a little comedy to their show, so they offered me a recurring spot. I auditioned for that one-day gig, and I ended up staying there, off and on, for three years. Three long runs: *The Sopranos*, *Rescue Me*, and now *The Good Wife*. What a feat for a stage manager from Brooklyn.

From the beginning, Mr. King and the writing staff introduced Howard as a man whose brain made a quick journey to his mouth and often, he was hilarious. He sat in on board meetings, joined in on some intimate sessions, interviewed new legal aides, and in general, was fun to be with. The cast included Archie Panjabi, Matt Czuchry, and Alan Cumming. The production had a two-month break at the end of every season which allowed all of us to fiddle around looking for vacation spots, have corrective surgeries long delayed or cameos then in production. Mark Saks, our casting director, found me a spot during my first break from *The Good Wife.*

I was delighted to take a one-scene cameo in *The Angriest Man in Brooklyn* because it starred Robin Williams, certainly the wildest man in Hollywood, and a talent worth watching in person. The action of the scene took place in a meeting of some sort (I never knew what the meeting was about since I never read the script and only had one line to speak) which was being chaired by Peter Dinklage, no less. It seemed Robin had been told by his doctor that he had but a few weeks to live because of Lewy body dementia. In retrospect, this was eerily and sadly ironic. It was a complicated scene, and it involved fast and furious dialogue between Robin and Peter along with single shots of the other actors in the scene, watching and interjecting quick lines of dialogue. Robin would entertain us whenever there was a break in the action. The scene began to reach an exhaustive peak, but he was never deterred from ad-libbing and rapid-firing verbal fireworks. Even during long rest periods in the makeshift green room, he continued while we all played at being a laughing audience. It was the most powerful hint of a man driven by some private and unconscious need to be *on* all the time. It turned out to be a very long day, but it was a memorable experience to have worked with such a rare talent, who could succeed in both comedic and dramatic roles, deeply moving fans across generations.

When I got back to *The Good Wife,* the writers had dreamed up a whacky one for me: Howard always slept in his undershorts on his couch during his lunch break every day, and insisted it kept his pants wrinkle-free and his shoes clean. This went on for a few episodes and made for a lot of fun. It was working because people stopped me on the street to inquire if I still wore underwear. It can be difficult to get a little comedy into a law office, but I think we did it. The production was like *Rescue Me* in that they had their own two-story building in Brooklyn and a courthouse a half-block away. Thanks to my seniority, I had a very comfortable dressing room right next to hair and makeup. I also had a van pick-up; I was really living the life of Riley.

On my second summer break from the show, Mark outdid himself and got me a Hallmark production filming in New Orleans. The script, a sweetly romantic tale, could have been written on a Hallmark card, but, hey, New Orleans is a city like no other and proved an excellent place to spend some time. They put Joan and me up at a Hilton near the Latin Quarter (Sylvester Stallone was staying there also, and never left the lobby as far as I could tell but sat there surrounded by some pretty tough looking guys). We had just missed Mardi Gras, but the town was still humming, and the restaurants had reservations available. I almost forgot I was there to work. In the film I played Sam, the proprietor of a jewelry repair shop, where our hero, Gus, worked. Gus, wonderfully played by Zachary Levi, had fallen for Molly, a waitress, and therein laid the problem. Gus had suffered a brain aneurysm some years before which left him unable to remember new faces from the day before, so he kept little notes reminding him of future dates. As usual, boy meets girl, boy loses girl, boy gets girl back with a little help from an aged Cupid— in this case, Sam, brilliantly played by me. Joan and I had a great time in the Big Easy and the production, slightly confusing as it was, was directed and played quite well. All in all, I remember it all—gastronomically.

Back at my other job, they had some seriously funny stuff for me to do. One of my favorite scenes is when I was interviewing new recruits for the firm and I got to play opposite America Ferrera, a truly gifted actress. It also was the season where Michael J. Fox joined the show. I'd like to share an example of his generosity: he arranged to have his company van include me in all pick-ups because he learned I lived somewhat near to him. We had many chats and it helped pass the time. On my days off, I auditioned for a role in a new drama being readied which had the interesting title, *Mozart in the Jungle*, and was about the experiences of the members of a classical symphony orchestra, loosely based on the life of the renowned conductor, Gustavo Dudamel. The character I read for was an aging trombonist who had been in the orchestra many years and was fighting to keep his place among the younger players. They asked me to take a few lessons on how to hold and play the instrument, which I did to absolutely no avail—it's a tricky and cumbersome thing that made me appreciate Tommy Dorsey even more. I eventually learned how to hold the thing, and so, on our next break, I took the part. Casting was complete with Gael García Bernal playing the conductor and Malcolm McDowell and Bernadette Peters also in the cast. It was a huge company filled out with actual musicians.

On the day of the shoot, I was ready for anything and took my seat between two pros to whom I explained my situation. The rehearsal went well, it was the same section of a Prokofiev piece I had learned earlier. Mr. Bernal had the same problem I did; he didn't know how to conduct, and I didn't know how to play the trombone. It must have been crazy to an onlooker as the music was sent into the auditorium and a real conductor, out of camera view, waved his baton so that Mr. Bernal could copy his motions while I imitated the trombonists at my side. We did the section many times until the director Paul Weitz was satisfied enough for us to start filming. It had been explained to me that during the music, my character begins feeling faint, and on a cue, they would stop, and put a stunt man in to do the fall. I insisted that I could do the fall, saving much time in stopping, putting the stunt man in, and continuing. Mr. Weitz had great trepidations about having an older man do the stunt, but he finally agreed it would enhance the scene. We already had plenty of cover up to the fall, so he showed me where and how to fall so he could get the best shot. There was a lot of suspense in the room, everyone hoping I wouldn't hurt myself. The scene started, I was doing well with the others but slowly seemed to be missing notes and on a cue, I fell off my chair, grabbed the mic stand next to me, and crashed out of view. The noise was deafening, then, the silence was total. As I rose, the director yelled, "*Cut!*" Then, he said, "terrific!," and everyone broke out into enormous applause. It was my first standing ovation!

There was another little scene in the hospital and after that I was approached by the producers, Jason Schwartzman and Roman Coppola, who asked if I would be interested in becoming a recurring character. I had already decided that the daily drive to the campus of SUNY, the University of New York at New Paltz, was hectic and the trombone was a pain in the ass. Now, if he played the piccolo . . .

Besides, I loved my job at *The Good Wife*. Unfortunately, the new season was to be its last. I was the King of Last Seasons: I had seen the end of *The Sopranos,* and the demise of *Rescue Me,* and now this. Everything was sadly closing down. A kind of ennui sets in with the writers and the regulars, who have been doing the show for years, as everyone begins seeking fresh material somewhere else and so it all falls apart. When it closed, it was still a favorite.

I enjoyed my time at home. Our building was on East 57th Street which ended in a little park overlooking the East River in New York City. It was great watching the ships go by and hearing the traffic overhead on the 59th Street Bridge. By the end of that summer, I was a contented man sitting in the park. And yet, I was beginning to get antsy as the weather turned colder and, as if on cue, Richard Schmenner of the New York Paradigm office called; there was an offer to do a film being shot in New York. I had been lying around, making Joan nuts for weeks, so if the part didn't require me to "lift heavy things," I assured him I was ready. The movie was titled *A Most Violent Year,* directed by J.C. Chandor. The cast was headed by Oscar Isaac, Jessica Chastain, and Albert Brooks: a first-rate group. The picture took place in and around Queens, New York in the violent eighties. Oscar's character, Abel, owns a heating oil business which was in competition with criminally owned operators hijacking trucks. They were all trying to gain a near monopoly in a lucrative business. I played a Hasidic rabbi, Josef, who owns a great deal of property left to him by his forebearers, one section of great value to Abel. In an opening scene, Josef is making a deal for the property with money down, and monthly payments until closing the deal in six months. If Abel defaults, he loses the deal and all monies involved. From there, the action of the movie circles around Abel fighting against all odds to raise the money and succeed. All my scenes were with Oscar, including the final scene where we close the deal. Happily, all these scenes were filmed with me sitting down, except the short scene where I appear in a limo. I had come to admire Oscar's work ethic, his preparation, and his talent. It was a great pleasure sharing a scene with him. What was not anywhere near a pleasure was the makeup involved in turning me into a Hasidic rabbi. Every day I was scheduled to work, it took over an hour, sitting in the barber chair while the makeup supervisor glued sections of hair to my face, neck and hairline. The glue was the kind we used for gluing model airplanes when I was a youngster. It also took an hour ungluing the hair pieces, saving them for the next tortuous day. Anyway, the movie was quite good with a load of action, J.C. was excellent and well-organized, and the movie did fairly well at the box office. It would do even better now that Oscar and Jessica are major stars. As for me, no one would know me with my disguise though I thought I was good in the film. At the wrap party, Jessica had no clue who I was until someone explained. Then I received a lovely greeting from her. It was truly a pleasure to be in a film with such fine actors as Jessica and Oscar.

When you get a message to help Larry David read his new play, *Fish in the Dark*, and are told that lunch will be provided, and that Tom Hanks will be there, you happily wonder: *why do they want me?* Of course, I accepted the invitation, but I hadn't seen him since I did *Curb Your Enthusiasm* over four years prior at that point and, as far as I could tell, he sure didn't need any help from me. I presented myself at the designated time and place, crammed full of questions, the main one being: *how in the hell could Larry David sit still long enough to write a play? A vignette, yes, but a real play?* The answer was forthcoming as I entered the room. The place was jammed full of actors, including the aforementioned Tom Hanks. Larry was with the exciting young director, Anna D. Shapiro, and the Broadway mogul, Scott Rudin. This was either some of the best actors in town joining together for one of the starriest casts ever assembled for a play, or Larry David was having lunch with a few friends. The reading was hysterical with the ad-libs flying by too fast to remember as the script was read by different actors in different roles. I had five lines in three scenes and got huge laughs for each one. I think I was the only one reading the Father part.

On the way home I recalled the only other time I was invited to read a new script. The older you get, the harder it is to remember names, so those of the screenwriter/director and title are a blank in my mind, but the names of the two actors reading with me were memorable: Al Pacino and Robert De Niro. The agency told me where and when I should meet them and to keep it quiet. We met in a room at the Actor's Studio and the two of them hugged and carried on. They finally settled down and we read the script, which was a total bore, but reading with two of the best actors on the planet was sensational. At the end, we all shook hands and, in the elevator, Pacino agreed with De Niro that the "script was crap." They got into a limo together and drove off. I walked home.

Cleverly, Ms. Shapiro got an audition from thirty actors in one fell swoop. The play called for a cast of fifteen and the final group came from that afternoon's reading, including me. With one exception: the role of the maid's young son in the play was cast later as Bobby Cannavale's talented son, Jake. Rehearsals began on February 2, 2015 at the newly renovated 42nd Street Studios. I had not done a Broadway play in three years, since *Taller Than a Dwarf*, and I sat amazed at how the art of stage management had progressed. I had won the Lifetime Achievement Award in Stage Management back in the seventies but Rolt Smith, our stage manager and his assistant, Julia P. Jones, ran circles around me, especially now that the iPad and the smartphone replaced my old mimeograph machine. All calls, script changes, and bulletins were sent out to our phones, and everyone was up to date on everything within seconds.

Ms. Shapiro was a genius in keeping order out of what could have been disorder. This was a zany farce and like all farces, it was hyper-realistic. She steered wonderful conversations on character development and inner needs and desires to the point where Larry felt he was a playwright not a comedy writer. We all joined in on the fun, and rehearsals, which could have been chaos, were a pleasure. For me, most of the fun was being involved in a Broadway play even though the play wasn't really a play. Oh, it had a beginning, a middle, and an end, and a director treating it as such, but it was really a vehicle designed to allow Larry David to appear, in person, before an adoring audience. The plot revolved around Sidney Drexel, the family patriarch, as he lay dying in a hospital. His sons and wife are fighting about who will be left most of the estate and Sidney's Rolex. Various family members arrive and join in on the arguments. There are the usual complications, all fast-paced and complicated, but *Fish in the Dark* was a uniquely funny and entertaining event.

We moved into the Cort Theatre and started previews in early March. By that time, the box office was so hot that we set a record in advanced sales before we did one preview showing Larry's extraordinary appeal and the affection audiences had for him. After some previews, we opened to mixed reviews but it didn't matter, people wanted to see him in person. Standing ovations every night and mobs waiting at the stage door for his autograph. My job was a piece of cake, two scenes from a hospital bed and rest for my bum leg. After a few months, Larry really had had it and discussions of closing before the originally advertised date began. He felt badly about the closing's effect on the cast, so he somehow seduced Jason Alexander to take over the role and give all of us a few more weeks of employment. Jason was absolutely amazing. He watched the show from out front and by the time he rehearsed with the full company, he was spot on. A date was set for Larry to leave and Jason to take over. *Fish in the Dark* was an event I wouldn't have missed for anything, even though it left me unemployed during the dog days of August. If you're not working or don't have a project in the works by the first of August, *relax*, nothing will happen for you until autumn. In Hollywood you can fill the time by doing a little networking in the casting offices, but in New York everything is done for you over your agent's telephone. Well, the phone didn't ring in August, either in New York or California. Though I wasn't supposed to, I did call Mark Saks, who said there was nothing going on, but rumor had it that there was a part in *The Good Fight* not going on for a month or so.

I was hanging around, enjoying theater with Joan, figuring the end of a career was near (I was in my mid-eighties by then, and who hires near nonagenarians?), when I returned an old phone message and got something interesting. The call was from Dr. Vincent J. Cardinal, artistic director of Connecticut Repertory Theatre and Chair of the Department of Dramatic Arts at the University of Connecticut. I called him back and apologized for the delay. I didn't tell him I rarely return calls from numbers I don't recognize, or that I was calling now, clearing messages with nothing else to do. Dr. Cardinale was terribly excited to talk to Hesh of *The Sopranos*, his favorite show. We chatted a while, mostly about my Honorary Doctorate of Fine Arts, which the university announced to be bestowed upon me in June. Imagine, me, never a Bachelor of Fine Arts, now a doctor. He explained, with the Dean's permission, that he would love to have me lecture the senior and junior classes on the art of auditioning and other aspects of employment in theater. I told him we would find an agreeable day. Not only did we find a day, I ended up with almost two years of working with seniors and juniors on auditioning and, of course, scene study. I was an Adjunct Professor in the Drama Department, working three days a week, living in our Connecticut place, and enjoying it.

Later, I got accidentally jostled in the subway in New York and fell down some steps, landing on the train platform, and cracking my left hip. Joan went for help while two policemen guarded me; while one handled the crowd, the other asked me for an autograph. The terrific EMTs got me to Roosevelt Hospital where after X-rays, the surgeon inserted some hardware, closing the crack. I spent a couple of weeks in rehab and finally hobbled home. "You're going to Israel, all expenses paid, you lucky duck," said Matt from Paradigm. I hadn't told anyone about my broken hip. So, who's going to Israel? Not me. I got mucho sympathy from the office: Wow, does it hurt? Are you in a cast? How did it happen? Are you suing? Is there anything we can do? I told them I could walk with a cane and I'm not suing because it was my own damn fault. Nothing fazes dear old Matt, and two weeks later he announced that he had resurrected the deal and that I shouldn't forget my passport. Incidentally, the show involved in all this was *Transparent*, an award-winning production starring Jeffrey Tambor, who played Maura, a transwoman, who came out later in life. In this episode, she takes the family to Jerusalem to find her long-lost grandpa, played by me. Everybody loved the cane as if they had thought of it themselves and was delighted to have me on board. With absolutely no resistance, they also agreed to having Joan come along as assistant to my lame leg. After all these years, I had hit the travel bonanza: a trip to Europe, first class for two, a hotel in Israel for as long as the company stayed there, and oh, don't forget the per diem.

I reported to the main stages of *Transparent* at Paramount and got a kick entering through the famous archway. There was no one at the office but I was directed to the most amazing encounter I had ever seen on a set. There was a wooden box in the middle of a huge group, who were treating the box as part of a religious ceremony. Joey Soloway, the show's creator, came over to greet me and they explained the group meeting which was part of the daily workload and that I would get acclimated as soon as the group finished the exercise. Joey had invented this group exercise in which anyone who so desires could stand on the box, in front of the entire company, and confess their innermost thoughts, desires, fixations or complaints. The group was made up of straights, queer, and trans folks, so the morning meeting was extraordinarily personal. After watching this tearful, cheerful, and lovely group, I finally met with Joey alone and during my time on the show, they became a close and dear friend. I can't say the same for Jeffrey Tambor, who saved his affections for Judith Light, a fine actress on the show, and for no one else, it seemed. The cast included Gaby Hoffman, Amy Landecker, Jay Duplass, and Kathryn Hahn, as just a few of the enormous and talented cast.

It was an amazing morning. We did a quick read-through and I happily got back to the hotel since I was first up, scheduled for a 6 a.m. pick up the next day. When I got off the elevator, I was greeted by Joan, sitting in the hallway. As if to answer my questioning look, she pointed to the door leading into our room. It seems the place had been taken over by the special effects people who were preparing me for a body makeover. I had no idea what a body makeover entailed, but it certainly sounded sinister. *Who set me up for it?* My permission was never asked for, nor given, but it was me they were after. Joan seemed to be enjoying the event— maybe she wanted one, whatever it was. All the furniture in the room had been pushed over to the windows, leaving a great space in the center, where a tent-like green structure loomed. It was explained that a spray of liquid sunshine was about to be applied to my naked body—I was supposed to be a fully sun-tanned Israeli. A discussion began as to what they really meant by "entire body." They intended to put me in the tent, naked as a newborn baby, and then hose me down like a tree on fire. I agreed to the basic intent, but no one was going to spray my privates. They had anticipated my timidity and produced a bikini of sorts and a headwrap. I entered the bathroom, undressed, changed clothes, and emerged— a giant Gunga Din. I thought Joan would have to be given CPR (cardiopulmonary resuscitation). When everything quieted down, I stepped into the lean-to and the crew began spraying me with a kind of liquid gold. It was the coldest shock I have ever known. Before I turned around, I was told the paint would dry completely before morning and the show would pay for the sheets I would ruin. All that done, they packed, replaced the furniture, folded their tent, and left. There I was, an Oscar award without the sword.

All of the indoor scenes and one scene at my character's seaside home in Jerusalem were shot in a beautiful place in Malibu with the intention to do the outdoor stuff in Israel as I show them the sights. My gimpy leg was holding up as the scenes by the Pacific were being done. My character was successful in the air-conditioning business and, as a result, rich, so rich that they hung enough gold jewelry on me to sink the Dead Sea. Suddenly, rumors were calling the trip off, as it was said the travel was too costly and some of the actors were reputedly afraid to fly. The final word came down just three days before we were scheduled to leave. I should have known the whole trip was like a pipe dream, gone in a wisp of smoke. At least the daily meetings allowed the group a powerful sense of being together. I wish every show had one.

It was obvious we had packed too heavily now that Israel was off the table, and, on account of the unexpected bad news, there was no B story ready to take over. Amazingly, the geniuses in the art department went to work, creating Israel in Hollywood. With very little budget to work with, they erected a replica Western Wall, a marketplace in Jerusalem, and a beach on the Dead Sea. If you happen to watch the last episode of season four, you would swear you were watching me escorting the group on a sight-seeing tour of Jerusalem. Truly *movie magic*. After those episodes were completed, we were flown back to New York.

If Brian Dennehy was willing to do a low-budget movie, I

certainly was. Having done studio-backed features and low budget indie movies, the differences could be labeled easily; there are the *majors* and the *minors*. In the *majors*, the script can take you anywhere in the world, the money is terrific, the perks are beyond fabulous, the craft food table is lavish, and the production assistants can't do enough to make you comfortable. In the *minors*, the money is the "low budget agreement," you get to the set by your own car or a company van, you bring your own lunch, and are met by a youngster banking enough hours so he or she can become a production assistant. The one element that makes the whole thing work, major or minor is talent. If there's enough of that lying around, nothing else matters. I thought *Driveways* had talent. Brian Dennehy and I were set as ex-soldiers living a quiet life and Andrew Ahn, our director, was exemplary. Christine Ebersole, from my *Camelot* days, a major talent, was there. The script was moody and warm-hearted about a mother, played by the lovely Hong Chau, and her son who arrive at her recently deceased sister's house. The boy, and later the mother, strike up a fond feeling for their neighbor across the driveway, Del, played by Brian Dennehy. Eventually Del becomes like a father to the boy. It is established during the action that Rodger, played by me, Del's VFW (Veterans of Foreign Wars) friend, is deep in the throes of dementia and has trouble remembering things such as picking Del up for their weekly shopping. One day at a bingo event, Rodger tells the group about a poem his high school teacher made them memorize, "Thanatopsis" by William Cullen Bryant, which keeps running through his mind. In spite of his dementia and loss of memory, he proceeds to recite the poem for all to hear. The poem fits the scene, as its title in Greek most nearly means a "view or consideration of death," and its text perhaps offers a sort of reverence for life and death, ruminating on how everyone dies, regardless of how great or small one is in life. It was quite difficult to memorize and perform directly into the camera lens. Here's the excerpt of the poem:

> So *live, that when thy summons comes to join*
> *The innumerable caravan, which moves*
> *To that mysterious realm, where each shall take*
> *His chamber in the silent halls of death,*
> *Thou go not, like the quarry-slave at night,*
> *Scourged to his dungeon, but, sustained and soothed*
> *By an unfaltering trust, approach thy grave,*
> *Like one who wraps the drapery of his couch*
> *About him, and lies down to pleasant dreams.*[16]

As you can see, the poem would be startling for anyone to rattle off, let alone a man in the late stages of Alzheimer's disease. I had great fun memorizing the piece, mainly to prove to myself that I was capable of doing it, even at my age; I was 89 years old at the time. *Driveways* turned out to be an affecting movie with an absolutely stunning performance by Brian Dennehy. Andrew Ahn took the film to the Berlin Film Festival where it premiered to much acclaim. Sadly, Brian passed away a month later, leaving us with a poignant farewell on screen. In his review for *Rolling Stone*, David Fear wrote of Brian's performance, "What we didn't know was that he had one last great turn in him before he'd be gone, one that would remind you of what an imposing presence and, paradoxically, a gentle giant he could be onscreen."[17]

A trio of excellent writers and producer/directors, namely

---

16 Bryant, William Cullen. 1821. "Thanatopsis" in *Poems*. Cambridge, Massachusetts: Hilliard and Metcalf.
17 Fear, David. 2020. "'Driveways' Review: Won't You Be My Neighbor?" *Rolling Stone*, May 14, 2020. https://www.rollingstone.com/tv-movies/tv-movie-reviews/driveways-movie-review-brian-dennehy-990230/.

Timothy Greenberg, Valerie Faris, and Jonathan Dayton, had a project in the works called *Living with Yourself*, which was to star Paul Rudd, a fine comedic actor. The story was about a writer in an advertising agency in the middle of a total writer's block who, after undergoing a mysterious treatment that promises him the allure of a better life, discovers that he has been replaced by a cloned version of himself. In a meeting with the group, they laid out the storyline and how the character they wanted me to play fit in. Knowing the technical difficulties that could arise from shooting such complex material, I was unsure, but they assured me my scenes were uninvolved with the movie magic necessary to pull off the sequences involving the clone. I signed on and did the scene a month later after they had a major part of the show in the can. In the show, I played an elderly European who had made a success of himself in America. The advertising agency had come to my baronial mansion to pitch some ideas for a future campaign, and I was listening with a friendly ear, eventually selecting Paul's character Miles's presentation. At the end of the meeting, my character arranges to be left alone with Miles. He initially seems a benevolent, kindly gentleman with a slightly Germanic accent, but as they begin their chat, things get darker as he relates an incident when he was imprisoned in a concentration camp during World War II; someone had stolen bread and he had pointed out the culprit who was immediately killed by the Nazi guards. "How did I know who had stolen the bread? I knew who had stolen the bread because it was me who had stolen the bread." It is a dramatic scene for me as I portray this event which ended with an ominous tone: don't screw around with this guy, he's more dangerous than he looks. The scene played well and fit in with Miles's general apprehensions. The series got good reviews, and Paul did yeoman work acting with himself, but the show strangely got little backing from Netflix and closed after one season.

Joey Soloway wanted me back in Los Angeles because they were doing a musical farewell to the Maura character and *Transparent*'s demise. They wanted all, or at least as many of the people who had been on the show as possible, to be there. I was hesitant to join in, figuring it certainly wasn't going to be a fond adieu to Jeffrey Tambor, who had single-handedly sunk the ship. I was wrong. Amazingly, Joey and their sister, Faith, had written an extraordinary musical tribute to Maura and a joyous celebration of love and loss. The piece began with Maura's death, and the family sitting shiva ends with the entire company singing and dancing in the woods near the Griffith Observatory and the Hollywood Hills. They had written the script dealing with the loss of a parent and the need to recover and survive, all with music and songs for each member of the immediate family. Altogether, it was a hugely reflective and joyous group. What a fabulous way to end the production. And yet there was more, a final group meeting. Everyone met on the empty Paramount stage and formed a great circle with the wooden box in the middle. There followed many personal confessions as those members from the circle, one after the other, gave thanks for being part of such a groundbreaking and memorable production. Joey gave a wonderful rehash of their experiences doing the long run and its sad finish without mentioning any names. They told of their love and respect for one and all. There was a tremendous reaction as they stepped down. Never in my memory, did a cast and crew give an ovation and show that amount of love; it was all proof of Joey's work ethic.

After that wonderful experience, I laid around for a few weeks; it was becoming obvious that my left leg was never going to heal completely from my bad subway fall. So, if casting needed a ninety-year-old with a limp—I was your man. Ironically, *Broad City* needed just such a person. It was a brilliantly zany show created by and costarring Abbi Jacobson and Ilana Glazer. I had recently been listed as one of the oldest working actors in the Actors' Equity Association, and so I was perfect casting as an old codger ready for some company. The episode's events take place after Ilana does an ancestry test and finds out she has a distant relative, played by me, who lives in Manhattan and is a Holocaust survivor. In an effort to learn more about her family's history of mental health for the personal essay portion of her grad school application, she and Abbi visit his assisted living home. Upon their arrival to the assisted living home, Abbi and Ilana discover that my character, Saul, yearns to spend the day outside of the home and, on top of that, desires new walking shoes. Despite rules regarding leaving the building, they wrap me in a carpet and sneak me out. There ensues an adventure through the city, including a drag brunch, stocking up at Zabar's, and a pit stop at DSW Designer Shoe Warehouse, where my character finds his desired set of shoes and exclaims, "Girls, I found it! A dope ass pair!" Eventually, we end up at Ikea, reflecting on the day over Swedish meatballs before heading back to the assisted living facility. In the end, my character has had the time of his life.

I had been trading emails with my dear friend, Peter Tolan, about the return of *Mad About You*, and by the summer of 2019 it had begun to look good. Peter was going to produce the venture, and he was letting members of the original production know that there could be a date announced for a fall start-up. It was now October and the rumors proved to be true. The agency called putting holds for a tentative rehearsal start in mid-November. It was fantastic reliving good times as the superintendent, Mr. Wicker. Strangely enough, I had kept my vest that I wore in every previous episode some twenty years ago. It had hung in the back of my closet looking brand new and, happily, it still fit.

It was totally weird the first day on the set, as it was the same apartment, repainted, of course, and with new furniture, but it looked almost identical. Paul had put on a little poundage and remarkably Helen looked about the same. Most of the cast was there: Anne Ramsay, Richard Kind, and John Pankow. The old camaraderie was everywhere, and it quickly felt like the years had done nothing to change the amazing fun we all felt doing the show. Add to that, we were a rarity, one of the few shows still being done with a live audience. It was the old schedule: Monday read-through and loose blocking, Tuesday read-through and loose run-through for the writers, Wednesday rehearsals and run-through for crew and producers, Thursday finalize script changes and camera blocking, Friday dress rehearsals and showtime. I strongly intended to do the show without my cane, as I managed to get through all the rehearsals without it. It was more tiring than usual, but my leg stood up through it all and that pleased me a lot. The show went well, and I shook hands all around, since I was only in the first two episodes. Joan and I decided to stay in Los Angeles for a while since it was close to the holidays, which we could spend with my daughters. We did all that and it was great fun. In early January 2020, there were rumors of dark days ahead. There was a terribly dangerous flu-like strain brewing in Washington state called COVID-19 and soon, rumors turned into fact. We decided to get back to New York and arrived just before the March 2020 lockdown. Everyone knows the rest of the story. Words will do it no justice.

And now, as the world seeks to find normalcy again, I look back at a miraculously long and fortunate career and I wonder: *what's next?* If nothing else, I'm endlessly grateful for the wonderful ride I've had.

First meeting for Fish in the Dark *with Tom Hanks & Rita Wilson*

Fish in the Dark *meets at Katz's Deli. Photographed by Jonathan Becker*

Me & Larry David at Citi Field when things were going better for the Mets

Guess who as Cardinal Benedetti in CSI

Epilogue

I told my grandpa that my niece Audrey is getting married. She and her partner are planning a lesbian wedding. Isn't that nice?

He said "It's a new world, *Mazel Tov*."

Great, because this woman could use some mazel, as she comes from a very dysfunctional family. Her brother ran away when he was fourteen years old, her mother sells dope to children in the school where she teaches, and her father is serving a life sentence at Sing Sing.

Grandpa said, "Never blame the child for the sins of the father."

Audrey's fiancée has a terrific job as a television producer. Grandpa quickly said "Television, that woman is in television? I will never speak to them again!"

Boy I am glad he doesn't know I am an actor.

Always good to end with a laugh.

Bibliography

Barnes, Clive. 1969. "Theater: 'The Madwoman of Chaillot' Set to Music; 'Dear World' Arrives at Mark Hellinger Angela Lansbury and Godreau Excel." *The New York Times*, February 7, 1969. https://timesmachine.nytimes.com/timesmachine/1969/02/07/77437919.html.

Barnes, Clive. 1972. "Stage: 'The Little Black Book' Opens." *The New York Times*, April 26, 1972. https://www.nytimes.com/1972/04/26/archives/stage-the-little-black-book-opens-benjamin-miss-seyrig-at-the-helen.html.

Barnes, Clive. 1973. "Theater: 'Good Evening.'" *The New York Times*, November 15, 1973. https://www.nytimes.com/1973/11/15/archives/theater-good-evening-zany-peter-cook-and-dudley-moore-return-the.html.

Bryant, William Cullen. 1821. "Thanatopsis" in Poems. Cambridge, Massachusetts: Hilliard and Metcalf.

Canby, Vincent. 1999. "From the Humble Mini-Series Comes the Magnificent Megamovie." *The New York Times*, October 31, 1999. https://www.nytimes.com/1999/10/31/arts/from-the-humble -mini-series-comes-the-magnificent-megamovie.html.

Conant, Jennet. 1996. "Heartthrob Hotel." *Vanity Fair*, December 1996. https://www.vanityfair.com/news/1996/12/george-clooney -199612.

Cookman, Anthony. 1955. "Whale of a Show." *Tatler & Bystander*, June 29, 1955.

Eder, Richard. 1979. "Stage: 'IRemember Mama.'" *The New York Times*, June 1, 1979. https://www.nytimes.com/1979/06/01 /archives/stage-i-remember-mama-with-liv-ullmann.html.

Fear, David. 2020. "'Driveways' Review: Won't You Be My Neighbor?" *Rolling Stone*, May 14, 2020. https://www. rollingstone.com/tv-movies/tv-movie-reviews/driveways-movie-review-brian-dennehy-990230/.

Gussow, Mel. 1971. "Theater: 'The Homecoming' Revived." *The New York Times*, May 19, 1971. https://www.nytimes. com/1971/05/19/archives/theater-the-homecoming-revived -janice-rule-and-tony-tanner-in-bijou.html.

Kerr, Walter. 1979. "Play: Gilroy Drama Of Me, 'Last Licks.'" *The New York Times*, November 21, 1979. https://www.nytimes. com/1979/11/21/archives/play-gilroy-drama-of-age-last-licks. html.

O'Connor, By John J. 1974. "TV: A Nicely. Done '6 Rrns Riv Vu.'" *The New York Times*, March 16, 1974. https://www.nytimes. com/1974/03/16/archives/tv-a-nicely-done-6-rms-riv-vu.html.

Paul Whiteman and His Concert Orchestra with Paul Robeson and Mixed Chorus. 1927. "Ol' Man River." B. Harms Co.

Rich, Frank. 1980. "Stage: Burton Stars in Revival of 'Camelot'; In King Arthur's Court." *The New York Times*, July 9, 1980.

https://www.nytimes.com/1980/07/09/archives/stage-burton -stars-in-revival-of-camelot-in-king-arthurs-court.html.

Schildcrout, Jordan. 2019. *In the Long Run: A Cultural History of Broadway's Hit Plays*. London, England: Taylor & Francis.. pp. 41-42.

Taylor, Markland. 2000. "Taller Than a Dwarf." Variety, March 13, 2000. https://variety.com/2000/legit/reviews/taller-than-a-dwarf -1200461160/.

Wilson, John S. 1970. "Hepburn's Hep but 'Coco' Isn't." *The New York Times*, February 15, 1970. https://www.nytimes. com/1970/02/15/archives/hepburns-hep-but-coco-isnt.html.

Jerry Adler is an American theater director, producer, and film and television actor. He is perhaps best known for his films *Manhattan Murder Mystery*, *The Public Eye*, *In Her Shoes*, and *Prime*. As well as his television work as Herman "Hesh" Rabkin on *The Sopranos*, he can be seen portraying Howard Lyman on *The Good Wife* and *The Good Fight*, building maintenance man Mr. Wicker on *Mad About You*, Bob Saget's father Sam Stewart on *Raising Dad*, Fire Chief Sidney Feinberg on *Rescue Me*, Moshe Pfefferman on *Transparent*, Saul Horowitz on *Broad City*, and Hillston on *Living with Yourself* with Paul Rudd. Jerry Adler resides in New York City with his wife Joan and their dog Hesh. He is presently working on a mystery novel due out in 2024. His debut memoir *Too Funny for Words* reflects his long and diverse career.